We need to make outreach part of the fabric of our congregations. This book offers a terrific pathway to lead your church toward a faithful fulfillment of the Great Commission.

—Lee Strobel, author, *The Case for Christ*

Outreach needs to be at the forefront of our mission and thinking, and Kevin Harney is a proven source for us to learn from. If you care about people who don't know Jesus yet, you have to read this book.

—Dan Kimball, author, *They Like Jesus but Not the Church*

There's nothing more important than building outreach-oriented churches, and there is perhaps no better coach to help you maximize your church's redemptive potential than Kevin Harney. I urge you to read this book.

—Mark Mittelberg, author, *Becoming a Contagious Church*

If you're looking for direction on how to instill evangelistic passion in your church, this is the book! *Organic Outreach for Churches* is a guide to creating a community that is all about helping others find their way back to God.

—Dave Ferguson, Lead Pastor, Community Christian Church

This book showcases a deep understanding of scriptural emphasis and teaching, the kind of practical help that comes only from real-life application, and an infectious pastoral passion that springs from the love of God first and a passion to reach the lost a close second. What a marvelous book!

—Gary Thomas

This eminently practical book shows how churches can change and become effective in outreach. The models presented here have been tested and found to work. An excellent resource for Christians longing to see renewal in their churches.

—Ajith Fernando, Teaching Director, Youth for Christ, Sri Lanka

Other Books in the Organic Outreach Series

Organic Outreach for Families

Organic Outreach for Ordinary People

DVD Curriculum in the Organic Outreach Series

Organic Outreach for Ordinary People (13 sessions)

Organic Outreach for Churches (10 Sessions)

Other Books by Kevin Harney

Leadership from the Inside Out

Seismic Shifts

Organic
OUTREACH
FOR CHURCHES

INFUSING EVANGELISTIC PASSION INTO
YOUR LOCAL CONGREGATION

Kevin G. Harney

ZONDERVAN

Organic Outreach for Churches
Copyright © 2011, 2018 by Kevin G. Harney

This title is also available as a Zondervan ebook.

Requests for information should be addressed to:
Zondervan, 3900 Sparks Dr. SE, Grand Rapids, Michigan 49546

This edition: ISBN 978-0-310-56607-6

The Library of Congress cataloged the original edition as

Harney, Kevin.
    Organic outreach for churches : infusing evangelistic passion into your local
congregation / Kevin G. Harney.
       p. cm.
    ISBN 978-0-310-27396-7 (softcover)
    1. Church growth. 2. Evangelistic work. I. Title.
    BV652.25.H367 2011
    266—dc23   2011027638

Cover design: Jay Smith at Juice Box Design
Interior illustration: Matthew Van Zomeren
Interior design: Ben Fetterley and Matthew Van Zomeren

Printed in the United States of America

HB 02.21.2023

Contents

Part 1
The Heart of Your Congregation

   Love for God is the foundation of organic outreach. If we fail to love God, he will not draw
   people to our church. When we love God passionately, he will entrust people to our congregation so we can lavish them with his grace.

   Any congregation that wants to reach out has
   to ask one simple question: what are we willing
   to sacrifice? Organic outreach will cost more
   than we dream, but it will be worth it!

   A joy-filled love for the church is also a key to outreach. If we don't love the church, why would our
   unbelieving friends love the Lord of the church?

Part 2
The Mind of Your Congregation

Part 3
The Hands of Your Congregation

Many of your best outreach programs are already in place; you just don't know it! Identify what you do well, and then turn your focus a few degrees out into the community and into the world.

There are countless ways to reach out and minister to your community. We need to be willing to risk failure to discover new levels of success.

Part 4
The Mouth of Your Congregation

There are countless places and ways to communicate the good news of Jesus. Every Christian in your church can be equipped to confidently share their testimony and God's story.

Acknowledgments

For two years, I had the opportunity to infuse the ideas found in this book into the DNA of a wonderful group of churches. They let me beta test the concepts of organic outreach and helped me refine the ideas found in the three Organic Outreach books in the laboratory of real churches. The staff and congregation of Shoreline Community Church in Monterey, California, have been the best laboratory imaginable for almost eight years. This congregation has modeled the ministry of Organic Outreach with deep passion and love and have seen hundreds of people come to faith in Jesus because of it. I am honored to be your pastor.

To the team at Zondervan: you have been amazing friends and partners in the ministry of publishing for more than two and a half decades. Finally, to my wife, Sherry, and my sons, Zach, Josh, and Nate: we have lived these truths together in the laboratory of our home, and now as my three sons have married and started their own homes. You are all examples of organic outreach.

Over the years, God has forged amazing partnerships with leaders and movements of Jesus followers who have embraced the vision of organic outreach. We are partners in the gospel, and each of you inspire me! I am honored to call you friends and colaborers.

- Dr. Ed Stetzer and Dr. Rick Richardson and the team at the Billy Graham Center for Evangelism
- Steve Murray and Rowland Forman and the leaders of Living Stones in New Zealand
- Dr. James Kraemer and all the district superintendents of the Church of the Nazarene

- Bruce Bugbee and the churches in the Far West Region of the Reformed Church in America
- Michelle Sanchez, Beth Seversen, and the churches that make up the Evangelical Covenant
- Jack DeVries and the leaders of the Christian Reformed Church of Australia
- Dr. Jim Dunn and the team at the Wesleyan Investment Foundation
- Kevin and Andrew Palau and the team at the Luis Palau Evangelistic Association
- Mary Schaller and the team at Q-Place

Introduction

Doctor, Doctor, Doctor:
Three Encounters with the Leaders of the
Billy Graham Center for Evangelism

STORY 1: DR. RICK RICHARDSON AND A GROUP OF LEAD PASTORS

Rick Richardson was leading the Billy Graham Center for Evangelism (BGCE), and he called me with a question. "We are using your book *Organic Outreach for Churches* as we train church leaders in evangelism. Could we bring you out to speak to some of the leaders we are training?" I was humbled and honored. I said yes.

In the middle of my teaching, one of the pastors raised his hand and interrupted. "It sounds like you are saying that evangelism should be the leading value in every church." I assured him that he was hearing me loud and clear. He reflected and then said, "I agree, but the truth is my prayer person thinks prayer should be the first value, my children's leader says children's ministry should be first, and my worship pastor thinks worship is first." Then he asked, "How do I get them to see that outreach needs to have a level of attention that is beyond any other area in the church?"

I had never been asked this question so clearly before. I pondered and then went rabbinical on him. Rabbis often answer a question with a question. So I invited all the pastors in the room to give an honest answer to the question I was about to ask. This seemed to get their attention.

I asked them, "If you stopped doing Sunday worship, had no music, no sermon, no corporate worship experience, how long would it be before people noticed and declared, 'Someone is not doing their job. We are not being the church'?" They thought for a moment and the first pastor said, "One week." The consensus around the room was that people in the church would rise up and express concern if there was no time or energy put into planning and executing a worship service for one week. I think there was one pastor who thought he might get away with it for two weeks, but that was the maximum. One or two weeks.

I pressed a bit more. "If you stopped doing discipleship and spiritual growth of believers at your church, how long would it be until your church members and leaders would rise up and say, 'We are not being the church'? If you stopped doing Sunday school, youth learning, Bible studies, and other forms of spiritual formation, how long would you get away with it?" Their answers ranged from two weeks to four weeks.

I looked at these gifted and passionate church leaders and asked, "If you did not do intentional evangelism, if you did not mobilize and equip your people to share their faith on a regular basis, how long would it be before your church noticed and complained?" The first person to respond was the pastor who had interrupted me. With sober and piercing honesty, he said, "Ten years and counting!"

There was a holy hush in the room. We did not know if we should laugh, cry, or do both. What followed was an honest discussion of why evangelism must be the lead value in every biblical church. The truth is, if it is not the first value, it will usually be the last (if it is a value at all).

STORY 2: DR. LON ALLISON AT THE NATIONAL OUTREACH CONVENTION

Almost ten years before I spoke to that group of leaders at the BGCE, I had another encounter. Lon Allison, the leader of the BGCE at that time, came up to me after I spoke at the National Outreach Convention. "You must write about these ideas and be a guest lecturer at our school," he told me. He was excited and affirming. He said, "You have an understanding of how to move a church toward evangelism that is desperately needed today."

I was flattered.

I was encouraged.

I was tempted to take him up on his offer.

Although I had been implementing these ideas in the local church for two decades, I knew I was not ready to share them in book form. I needed to do more work, pray more, and test these concepts in multiple settings with a variety of leaders.

At the same conference, I had lunch with Lee Strobel and Mark Mittelberg, two of the most powerful leaders and evangelists I know. They also challenged me to get my ideas out to the church as soon as possible. I respect both of them but still resisted the idea of writing a book about outreach. I knew there were things I needed to learn, test, and refine.

My caution in writing this book was based on my concern that Christian authors and publishers can be quick to roll out ideas and approaches that have not been adequately field-tested. We tend to take concepts that work in one setting and quickly tell every church that will listen, "This will work for you, at your church, and in your context." I have seen this cause discouragement and pain for many leaders and congregations.

I did not want to make this mistake.

Instead of writing a book on evangelism, I committed to lead outreach in two more congregations. I also found leaders from nine churches who would let me mentor them for two years and use their churches as laboratories for the ideas in this book. This gave me eleven distinct ministry settings in which we could examine, test, and refine these concepts. In the process, we discovered things that work, and we identified a number of ideas that are not effective or do not translate well to diverse ministry contexts. We learned a lot!

The churches I worked with ranged from a church-plant of about a hundred people (more than half under the age of twelve) to a large multisite congregation with more than five thousand people attending weekend services. They represented various denominational and theological backgrounds, ranging from Wesleyan to Reformed. The outreach leaders I trained were men and women, volunteers and paid staff, lead pastors and support staff.

I met with these leaders monthly to pray, train, get feedback, and engage in a process of mutual learning. I took all the ideas I thought would be broadly transferable and tested them over and over.

Together we weeded out what did not work. We reinforced what was effective. We struggled with and thought deeply about how a congregation could learn to organically reach out. We identified roadblocks and removed them. And we saw churches reorient their focus to the biblical call to "make disciples of all nations."

Five years after the conference where I was exhorted to write this book, I finally felt ready. But I have to be honest; I have not perfected all of these ideas. I am still a student of evangelism, and I always will be. I don't pretend that every idea in this book will work perfectly in your ministry setting.

I am confident that these concepts and ministry tools will help most churches take significant steps in their efforts to reach out with Jesus' love and grace. I can tell you that everything in this book has been field-tested and has borne tremendous fruit in a variety of congregations. I can assure you that these ideas have been born of deep time in prayer. I can promise that the members of the Outreach Influence Team that worked with me on the content of this book love Jesus and are laboring in churches that are reaching out with ever-increasing effectiveness. I can offer this book knowing that it is biblical to the core. I am confident that if your church seeks to use the ideas in this book to shape the future of your ministry, lost sheep will come home to the Great Shepherd, and the angels of heaven will join with your congregation in the celebration.

STORY 3: DR. ED STETZER AND THE FUTURE

Today we are seeing evangelistic leaders around the United States and the world seeking a new level of partnership, common vision, and collaboration. Ed Stetzer is now leading the BGCE (at the time that the Organic Outreach trilogy of books was being rereleased). He feels a unique call to gather evangelism leaders through a scholars group as well as influential denominational and movement leaders. I have the honor of partnering with him and a number of other leaders in this new season of focus on mobilizing the church to be a powerful hub of evangelism all over the world. I believe God is preparing the church for a new revival of evangelistic fruitfulness.

Since this book was first released, my wife, Sherry, and I have cofounded a ministry called Organic Outreach International (www .organicoutreach.com) in partnership with Shoreline Community Church. This ministry is working with churches, movements, and denominations in places like Sri Lanka, the Ukraine, Canada, New Zealand, Australia, the United States, and many more. The ministry of Organic Outreach International is influencing more than twenty thousand churches around the world (that we know of). The executive pastor of Organic Outreach International, Walt Bennett, is helping us forge new partnerships and ministry alliances on a weekly basis. The vision of helping churches and Christian ministries move outward with the good news of Jesus in natural ways is becoming a reality!

We are so committed to this vision that we seek to give away everything we can. On the Organic Outreach website you will find teaching videos, inspirational video stories, three years of curriculum to guide a church through an organic outreach transformation, and much much more! These are all free. Please take a few minutes to explore the website. You will be amazed at all that we have there, and the resources are in English and in Spanish!

We are also developing and equipping coaches, cohort leaders, and training events that are being held all around the world. These are all designed to help churches maintain the evangelistic momentum that seems to die out after about thirty days.

All of these tools work only when we realize that outreach is not simply about sending money and prayers to the mission field on the other side of the planet (though this is a good thing). We don't reach our full evangelistic potential just by having a committee that plans occasional events to reach out (though this can be very helpful). Organic outreach is what happens when evangelistic vision and action become the domain of every ministry in a church and the commitment of every member of a congregation.

This will not happen accidentally. There will be huge spiritual resistance to outreach. The only way outreach will become a natural part of a congregation's life is when every leader and each ministry is gripped by a commitment to fulfill the Great Commission. When this happens, outreach will not be an add-on or an occasional ministry project. It will become part of the very culture of the church. This is what I mean by *organic*. It is a natural and integrated part of the whole life of the church, not an add-on.

Engaging in outreach organically will look a little different in each church. Every congregation has a personality, style, and vibe. But regardless of context, outreach should always flow naturally from a church that loves and worships God. Outreach should be the heartbeat of every church. It should never be an afterthought.

Organic Outreach for Churches provides direction for congregations that want to graft evangelistic passion and practice onto the DNA of their churches. This book is designed to help your church find organic ways to connect with your community, share Jesus' message, and point people to the Savior of the world. It will take time, it will mean sacrifice, and it will drive you to pray with greater passion, but you will see a harvest of eternal fruit.

I invite you to receive from the work I have done. I also hope you will become my teacher. Join in the conversation, take action, and together we can continue the amazing work of taking Jesus' love, grace, and message from where we are to the ends of the earth.

Part One

THE HEART
OF YOUR
CONGREGATION

Why does God draw people to a particular church? Have you ever asked yourself why God would bring people to the church you attend? Have you ever been apprehensive about inviting a friend or neighbor to your church? Has it ever crossed your mind that God might actually be keeping people from your church?

These are important questions.

God is absolute and pure love.[1] He loves people with passion, tender mercy, and amazing grace in ways that we can't fully comprehend. When Jesus was asked to identify the greatest and most important of all the commandments, he pointed to God's call for us to love.[2] We are to love God with everything we have and to love other people the way we long to be loved.

If a congregation is gripped by God's love and lavishes it freely on each other and their community, God will draw people to this church. God is the one who draws people and softens hearts. He is also the one who will stop spiritually curious people from coming to a church that will not introduce them to the amazing grace and love of Jesus.

This means we need to do a spiritual check on our congregation's heart. Does our heart, as a church, beat with the love and compassion of the living God? Can people see our compassion? Can they feel it? Are we fulfilling God's call to lavish him, each other, and our neighbors with love?

Chapter One

Loving God

Without This, Nothing Else Matters

Love for God is the foundation of organic outreach. If we fail to love God, he will not draw people to our church. When we love God passionately, he will entrust people to our congregation so we can lavish them with his grace.

A person is lying on a surgical table. It's the moment of crisis. Doctors and nurses are working frantically to save a life. But it's clear they are losing their patient. Next to the operating table, the EKG shows the patient's heartbeat.

It is erratic.

It is fading.

It is gone.

A loud, high-pitched drone sounds, and a flat line appears on the monitor.

The heart has stopped.

Instead of giving up, the medical team increases its activity. The head doctor calls for a crash cart. Paddles are amped up with electrical current and pressed against the patient's chest. The doctor calls, "Clear!" and shocks the patient's heart.

All eyes again turn toward the monitor with anticipation, fear, and hope.

Nothing.

Still, the doctor is not ready to give up.

"Clear!"

Again, current is sent through the heart. All eyes turn toward the monitor. A flat line is all they see, and the high-pitched drone is still all they can hear.

Then, after what seems an eternity, a single beep. Suddenly, there is an upward line on the monitor. Then another, and another. The heart is beating once again.

Blood is flowing.

A life has been saved.

WHEN GOD LOOKS AT YOUR HEART

When God looks at his bride, the church, he longs for her to have a healthy heartbeat. He wants our hearts to beat with his love for the lost, and he longs for evangelistic passion to flow through our veins. The Maker of heaven and earth wants to see each and every church alive with love for the lost and engaged in reaching out with the message and grace of Jesus in natural, organic ways.

God wants to draw people into our fellowship with the assurance that they will be embraced by grace and introduced to the Savior, Jesus. But this can happen only when the people in our church are deeply in love with God.

When we are, our heartbeat is strong.

When we do not love God, it is difficult for us to love others.

As God looks at the spiritual monitor that registers the evangelistic heartbeat of a church, he sees one of several different patterns. What do you think God sees when he looks at your church?

FLAT LINE

Some churches have a loud, high drone and a flat line on their heart monitor. There is no love for God, nor is there a relentless love for the lost. These churches are closed off to visitors, their community, and the world. They don't reach out or train their members to share Jesus' love. Prayer for their community is nonexistent. There was a heartbeat at some time in the distant past, but today the church is flatlining.

If this describes your church, don't lose hope! We believe in a God who can raise the dead. Heaven is watching your church's heart monitor, and the Spirit of God is always ready to send a pulse of heavenly energy into your congregation's heart to bring it back to life. There are tools God can press against your heart to bring a new season of evangelistic life to your church. God is ready to return your church to her first love, Jesus Christ.[1] And the Holy Spirit is ready to move your church from apathy to passion.[2]

WEAK PULSE

Sometimes when a doctor checks for a pulse, he'll say, "I have a pulse, but it's weak." There is still life in the body, but action needs to be taken quickly to sustain it.

Many churches have a pulse and there is life, but it's faint. There is love for God and for people, but it is waning.

If this is a picture of your church, be honest and admit it. You might have a map on a wall somewhere with several pins showing where you send money to support missionaries. You might do an event or two each year that "spiritual seekers" are welcome to attend. You might even try to be friendly if a guest or visitor happens to wander into your church on a Sunday morning.

But honestly, your passion for outreach is gone.

Your church lacks a desperate love for God that will drive you into the world with his good news. You are nice to people who visit your church, but you don't go out of your way to reach those who are far from God. You send money overseas, but you don't engage the mission field right next door.

If this describes your congregation, you too need to fall in love with God — Father, Son, and Holy Spirit — all over again. Yes, you still care. You love God, and you love people. But it is time to rehabilitate your congregation's heart.

Some key exercises can fortify your heart and make it beat strongly again. The heart is a muscle, and if you exercise it, it becomes stronger. There are ways you can strengthen your church's heart, practical things you can do to increase your love for God and for the world. At the end of each chapter of this book, you will find some activities designed for that purpose.

RAPID HEARTBEAT

Sometimes a heart races wildly. This can be very dangerous, because if a person's heart pumps too fast for too long, it can lead to cardiac arrest and eventually death.

Some churches' monitor shows that their heart is beating two or three times faster than a healthy heart. Because these churches love God and want to be faithful to his love for lost people, they launch outreach program after outreach program and initiative after initiative. Church members grow tired and exhausted, as the congregation jumps into the latest evangelistic fads.

Outreach is not organic in a church like this. Instead, it feels fabricated and inauthentic. While the motives are right, the practice of outreach is so forced that it fails to bear much fruit. Churches like this often experience frustration when they try lots of programs but never find something that works. They invest lots of money and time, and they genuinely love God, but lost people rarely come to know and embrace Jesus.

Some years ago, my brother-in-law ended up in the hospital because his heart started racing. It wouldn't stop, and the doctors found that it was beating far too rapidly. Eventually, a medical team had to shock his heart to slow it down to a healthy rhythm. When the medical team pressed the paddles to his chest and sent an electrical current through his body, his heart slowed and once again beat at a normal pace.

Some churches need to love God enough to slow down. If they want to establish an organic culture of outreach, they need to do *less* to accomplish more. Better yet, they need to channel their energy, time, and resources into a sustainable approach to churchwide evangelism. Whatever the condition of your church's heart, know that God is ready to increase your love quotient. Evangelism is not a sprint; it's a marathon. It's not a fad; it's the fabric of a healthy church. It is not a system or a program; it's the natural fruit of a church that loves God.

GETTING BACK TO YOUR FIRST LOVE

The first and most critical step a church needs to take to move toward healthy outreach is to develop a growing love for God. In the book of Revelation, Jesus says to the church of Ephesus, "Yet I hold this against you: You have forsaken your first love."[3] Whenever our love for God ceases to be first place in our hearts, our vision for reaching out wanes.

Jesus made this clear when he taught his disciples that the first and most important of all the commandments is to "love the Lord your God with all your heart and with all your soul and with all your mind and with all your strength."[4] This is not just our calling as individual followers of Christ; it is also our calling as a church. If we forget our first love, our collective heart will grow cold, and nothing that we do will have the impact we desire.

Loving God does not begin with our own efforts. It is based on the awareness that God was passionately seeking us long before we ever sought him. In the letter of First John, we find a powerful tutorial on the love of God. We learn, first and foremost, that God is love. Because of his love for us, we can become children of God. The depth of the Father's love was revealed when he sent his only Son to this earth to die in our place, on the cross, for our sins. As we are grounded in God's love for us and as we learn to walk in this love, we will continue to grow in our love for people and for God.[5]

If your church is struggling to invest in reaching your community and the world, ask yourself this question: are we a church that is on fire with a passion for God? If reaching out to others has been pushed to the back burner (or off the stove entirely), it probably won't help to add some spice to the meal. You need to start by turning up the heat.

Maybe your church has lost its first love.

Remember, God so loved the world that he *gave*.[6] Love gives. And when a congregation's heart pounds hard for God, we give of ourselves—our time, our resources, our lives—to love others.

Heart healthiness begins as we examine our love for God, both as individuals and as a church. And as we rediscover our first love—our passion for God—we repent and begin to do the things we used to do. We begin to love the world again and find our hearts stirred with longing for people to meet the great Savior who has changed our lives.[7] Reaching out to the lost with love is the organic overflowing of a heart that is intimate with God.

ORGANIC GARDENING

PREPARING THE SOIL

Gather a group of your church's leaders and influencers to do a heart check. This group can include board members, Sunday school teachers, youth volunteers, staff, and anyone who helps give direction to the church. Read this chapter together and have an honest conversation about the heartbeat of the church. Focus on your church's love for God and how this impacts your love for those who are not yet part of God's family.

Identify whether your church's heartbeat is flatlining, weak, rapid, or healthy.

- If your heartbeat is flatlining, talk about ideas for shocking your church with a pulse of heavenly energy to get the heart beating again.
- If you have a weak pulse, identify a couple of ways you can strengthen your heart.
- If you have a rapid heartbeat, identify what things you are doing in the area of outreach that are the most organic and fruitful. Be willing to set some things aside for a season and to learn to do fewer things in a better way.
- Was there a time in your history as a church when your heartbeat was strong and your love for God was more passionate? What can you do to recapture that spirit in this new season?

- When your congregation gathers to worship, what are some of the ways that you express a passion for God? What can you do to grow as worshipers?
- If your heartbeat is healthy, spend time thanking God for this and identify how you can maintain this healthiness.

Pray together and ask God to help your church increase your heart's healthiness so that you will move boldly into the world with Jesus' love and message.

SCATTERING SEEDS

One of the best ways to grow your congregation's heart for God is worship. Consider planning a special worship service to celebrate the love, grace, and goodness of God. Plan according to what connects for your congregation, but make it exciting and thoroughly God-centered. Invite your congregation to gather to praise, worship, and celebrate the one who made them, loves them, and is always with them.

WATERING WITH PRAYER

- Pray for the heartbeat of your congregation to be healthy.
- Ask the Holy Spirit to deepen your love for God.
- Use Revelation 3:14–22 to guide your time of prayer.
- Confess where your own heart has grown cold and pray for a fire to be ignited in it.
- Ask Jesus to fill your church so full that his love overflows from your hearts to those who do not yet know his love and grace.

Chapter Two

Loving the World

What Are You Willing to Sacrifice?

Any congregation that wants to reach out has to ask one simple question: what are we willing to sacrifice? We never compromise on God's Word or the core beliefs of the faith, but if we are going to reach the world with Jesus' message, there will be a price. Organic outreach will cost more than we dream, but it will be worth it!

I have trained church leaders on evangelism in many different churches, denominational gatherings, national conferences, and international settings for more than two decades. In almost every context, one question always comes up. At some point, as I am teaching, an exasperated and discouraged leader will ask me, "What will it take for our church to turn the corner? How can we engage in outreach that will actually change lives in our community?"

As they share their story, they often tell me about various efforts they have made, prayers they have offered, money they have spent, staff they have hired, and programs they have implemented. The result is always the same: very little kingdom fruit. They are passionate about the gospel, but something has gone wrong. They sense there is something in the culture of their church that is working against effective outreach.

I often respond to their question by sharing three critical pieces of the ministry puzzle, pieces that must be in place in a congregation for it to turn the corner and become an outreach church. I assure them that if they can say an enthusiastic and honest yes to three questions, they are well on their way to witnessing an outreach explosion in their community.

I also warn them that if they answer an honest no to any of these three questions, it will be difficult to develop a culture of organic, life-changing outreach in their church.

At this point, I have their attention. People love it when you can give them steps to success, and most people think that is what I am about to offer them.

I wish it were that simple.

Sadly, there are *not* three simple steps to effective evangelism.

Instead, I offer them three building blocks that help cultivate a culture that invites evangelistic movement, three primary things a church must value and embrace if they really want to see the good news of Jesus impact their community and the world.

THE THREE CRITICAL QUESTIONS

Question 1

Does your church believe, honor, and follow the teaching of the Bible?

If a church has forsaken the Bible and does not believe what the Scriptures teach about sin, heaven, hell, and the saving power of Jesus alone, there is little chance they will ever have an effective, organic outreach.[1] If they have forsaken the truth of the Bible, it's unlikely that outreach will ever be a consuming passion.

A church might make an effort to keep from shutting their doors. They might want to grow. They might even be willing to implement tactics to engage new people. But only a desire to see people repent of sin, enter a life-giving relationship with Jesus, and be born again through his sacrificial death on the cross will lead to a lasting evangelistic movement in a congregation.

The truth and authority of the Word of God are a church's backbone. A congregation will follow what God says — even when it is hard — as long as its members know that God's Word clearly calls them to reach out to the lost, to sacrifice their time and resources, and to winsomely share Jesus' message with others.

Your congregation must be committed to the truth and authority of God's Word. The Bible is a powerful means of challenging people who typically do not want to try new things or take risks. A congregation that is wholeheartedly devoted to following the teachings of Scripture will inevitably be propelled beyond what *they* want in order to become what God is calling them to be. If the members of your church are willing to embrace the Word of God as truth and as their roadmap for life, there is still hope that they can be led into world-changing outreach.

Question 2

Does your church love people and long for them to know Jesus?

When a congregation is in love with itself and is committed to self-preservation, it's unlikely it will count the cost and take steps to reach out. But when the people in your church truly love others, that love drives them outward. When they love people so much that they hurt over their lost condition, they will do whatever it takes for those they love to taste the goodness of the gospel and to experience the love of God.

As the members of your church listen to the voice of Jesus saying, "Love your neighbor as yourself," they will be compelled to look beyond the walls of the church and the circle of their church family. Love, inspired by the Spirit of God, propels us out of our comfort zones and into the world.

After I share these first two questions, most of those listening are nodding their heads in agreement. This is particularly true when I interact with believers from more traditional congregations that preach the Bible faithfully and have been committed to world missions for many years. Most of them are thinking, "Yes! We are two for two! Our church is committed to both of these." I even get an occasional bold "Amen!"

Then, I ask the third question.

Question 3

Are the people in your church willing to sacrifice to the point that they will joyfully embrace change?

After I ask this question, the atmosphere in the room usually changes. Many of the people who were excited shrink back. They shift in their chairs and look uncomfortable. I see concern on their faces. Some even groan out loud. It's as if the oxygen has been sucked out of the room and people are gasping for air. I'm not exaggerating.

I have met with leadership teams of churches all around the world and have asked these three questions over and over again. I find that many churches can confidently say, "We believe and hold to the Word of God, and we believe the gospel, love people, and want to reach out." But when it comes to the idea of changing, people seem to hit a brick wall.

They want to reach out but fear the cost of even suggesting change to the congregation. They love people outside of the church, but not enough to risk incurring the wrath of members who like things just the way they are. They believe the Bible is true, but they are not willing to take up their crosses, deny themselves, and follow Jesus into a lost and broken world.[2]

Cultivating a culture of organic outreach in your congregation requires making strategic changes to orient your vision and practice around the Great Commission. Outreach can't be only the work of a committee or just a yearly weekend emphasis. It's not enough to give money to missionaries and pray for others to reach the world.

Outreach must be woven into the culture of a church, into every aspect of its life and ministry. Only when a church grafts evangelistic passion onto every ministry will outreach become more than just another program. But this won't happen if you want things to stay the same. And change requires sacrifice.

EVERY CHURCH IS COMMITTED TO OUTREACH NO MATTER THE COST, RIGHT?

Ask any pastor what their church values most. Somewhere near the top of the list they will probably say, "Outreach!"

"We want to be a church that reaches our community."

"We are committed to the Great Commission."

"Our church wants to serve and love people in our community in a way that will bear witness to the love and presence of Jesus."

If their words don't convince you, they may produce a church vision statement that clearly lists evangelism, outreach, proclaiming, or some similar concept to show you that it is a core value of the church.

There you have it.

This is a church that is committed to outreach.

I've found that this declared commitment to evangelism is almost universal in the church. You would be hard-pressed to find a church that says, "We don't believe in outreach. As a matter of fact, we stand aggressively against evangelism."

So let's be clear: the issue is not whether a church lists outreach as a priority on its website or in its purpose statement. The issue is not even whether a church makes some type of outreach effort. Most congregations can point to at least some form of evangelistic activity going on in their church.

The real issue facing the Western church today is that the efforts of very few churches are actually bearing fruit. Many churches have hit a growth plateau or are in decline.[3] They want to reach out, but they are not willing to pay the price. They are not willing to count the cost.

LOVE THE WORLD

The Bible tells us that Jesus loved the world. He saw people as they really were, lost and dead in their sin and brokenness, and yet he still cared for them and sought them out. If a church wants to reflect Jesus' heart and mission, it also must learn to love the world that Jesus died to save.[4]

In the early 1990s, Corinth Reformed Church contacted me three times over the course of three weeks and asked me to consider being their lead pastor. Every time, I gave them the same response: "No."

You would think they'd finally take the hint, but apparently I wasn't being clear enough for them. The week after my third no, a member of the search team called and asked if he could bring a few people over to my home to talk with me. Once again, I let them know that I was not looking for a new church to serve. But he persisted and asked if I would just give them an hour of my time to share what I thought about their church. They asked me if they could pick my brain and learn from me. I finally agreed to meet with them.

Later, I realized they were being very sneaky!

The day they came over to talk with me was my day off, so I was in jeans and a wrinkled In-N-Out Burger T-shirt.

My wife asked me, "Aren't you going to change?"

I told her that I had made it clear that this was my day off, that this was not an interview, and that I was doing them a favor. So I was staying in my "day-off uniform."

Three of Corinth's members showed up and we had a great chat. They asked me lots of questions, mostly about how I thought people perceived their church. I asked them if Corinth Church was a body of believers that was ready to count the cost, make sacrifices, and do whatever it takes to reach the community with the grace of Jesus. Keep in mind that this church had been around for a full century and in all that time had grown from a few people to slightly less than three hundred members. In other words, they had a growth rate of about three people a year, mostly as a result of births and marriages. In fact, a good portion of the church was made up of just three large extended families. Now, don't misunderstand me; these were wonderful people. They believed in the Bible. They cared about the community. They wanted to reach out with the love of God.

The problem was that they were not quite sure what to do next. I assured them that committing to evangelism would cost them more than they realized. They insisted that they were ready to count that cost. After talking for about an hour, we prayed, and they headed for the door.

As the last member of this little group was walking out, he stopped, looked me straight in the eyes, and said, "You are not hearing God, and you need to pray more." Then he left.

Let's just say that I was a bit irritated by his declaration.

I told my wife what he had said and how it bothered me. Her response was not what I wanted to hear. She thought about it for a moment and said, "Well, maybe you *should* pray more."

Since my wife is right (most of the time), I actually did take some more time to pray, and I agreed to visit Corinth Church, preach on a Sunday morning, and take a posture of openness to any nudgings of the Holy Spirit. I also told the search committee that I wanted an opportunity to interview the congregation.

They weren't quite sure what I meant, so they asked me to explain. I told them I wanted them to gather all of the adults in the church, from high school students to senior citizens, and let me talk to them. I wanted a full hour to share what the Bible says the church is supposed to be. I also wanted to ask them questions about their commitment to reach their community and the world with the good news of Jesus. In short, I wanted to find out, firsthand, just how much they were willing to sacrifice for Jesus.

At this point, I was fairly sure that I was *not* going to become the pastor of this small country church in Byron Center, Michigan. As I interviewed the congregation (about 75 percent of the adults were there that morning), I was direct. I asked if they were really ready to sacrifice for the sake of the gospel. I held up my Bible and said to them, "The church should never compromise on this. Everything else is up for grabs!"

They agreed. They assured me, once again, that short of compromising on the Word of God, they were ready to do whatever it would take to reach their community for Christ. So I explained, in detail, what this would mean. I asked if they were ready to give up some of the shape, form, and style of worship that had been the norm for almost a hundred years. I asked if they were ready to set aside their personal tastes for the sake of reaching new people. I reminded them that this was not their church, that it was Jesus' church, that anyone who might come to the church was an invited guest. In particular, I asked if they were ready to welcome a new person, with no spiritual heritage or history, into the church family as a full member. I asked if they were ready to treat a brand-new person the same way they treated a lifelong third-generation member. I asked them if we could move the furniture in the sanctuary, if we could change the service times, if we could revise the order of worship (which had not been significantly altered for decades), and if they were willing to give their finances for ministries that were focused not on them or their family members but on people in the community.

I fired everything I had in my arsenal. I pushed and prodded. And when I was done, I gave them permission to write me notes to let me know why I should *not* be their pastor.

To my amazement, I was flooded with letters from these dear people saying, "We believe God wants you to come to lead this church."

They really thought they were ready to make the sacrifice.

But I was still doubtful.

ONE YEAR LATER

As you may have guessed, I accepted the call to be their pastor. Almost a year later, a friend asked me, "What has been the biggest surprise of your ministry so far?"

Without hesitating, I said, "They told me the truth!"

I had heard countless horror stories from pastors who had been in situations just like mine. They had been invited by an enthusiastic search committee claiming they wanted to reach outside of the church, only to discover that the congregation disagreed (in theory or in practice). In most cases, the disconnection between the pastor's expectations and the congregation's desires had led to painful battles and resistance every time the pastor tried to lead the congregation to pursue a more externally focused vision for the church.

Thankfully, that was not my experience at Corinth Church. For the next dozen years, the congregation willingly made sacrifices and counted the cost to reach out. And the results were (and still are) glorious! Hundreds and hundreds of people came to faith in Jesus. The church doubled in size, then doubled again, and is continuing to grow and reach out. Much of this increase has been through brand-new believers coming to know God's love.

They have counted the cost, over and over again. They have sacrificed. They have been like Jesus.

HUMBLE HEARTS AND HEROIC SACRIFICES

Nancy looked at me as we met in my office at the church and said with humble honesty, "I don't like the new worship music. I don't like the guitar. It does not help me worship. I just don't like it. I like the old music, the hymns. I like when the organ plays."

This conversation was a bit awkward for me because I had been the worship leader the previous day. I also happened to be the one playing the guitar. So I asked her to clarify what she wanted me to do. "Nancy, do you think we should use only the organ and get rid of the guitar? Do you think we should change back to the old music, to the kind you like?"

She was quick to reply. "Oh no! I think we *should* use the guitar music. It will help us reach some of the young people and draw new people to the church. I just wanted you to know that I don't enjoy it."

I had to chew on this for a moment before I understood what she was saying. And then I realized why she had wanted to meet with me. It wasn't to gripe about the worship service. Nancy was telling me, in a roundabout way, "I am willing to sacrifice what I love for the sake of reaching others."

She was letting me know that she wanted to be like Jesus.

She was sacrificing her desires for the sake of the gospel.

She just needed her pastor to know that even though she was willing to pay the price to reach the lost, it still hurt.

That meeting with Nancy was a huge moment for me in my ministry. I realized that this dear servant of Jesus was doing exactly what the congregation had promised me they would do. She was sacrificing for the gospel.

I blessed her and thanked her. It was the first of hundreds of moments in the coming years when people at the church laid down their tastes and desires for the sake of the gospel.

Any church that takes outreach seriously will quickly learn that sacrifice is essential. Just as Jesus left the glory of heaven, emptied himself, and was willing to suffer to bring grace to this lost and broken world, we also must sacrifice and suffer to share his good news with others.[5]

WHAT WE HAVE, WHAT THEY HAVE

It was wonderful to have Nancy share with me that she was willingly choosing to sacrifice for the sake of reaching out. But there also were people who were not quite as willing to pay the price. Every so often someone would come to me and say, "Pastor, I am all for this reaching out stuff, but be sure you don't forget us!" They still had this strange idea that if the church was focused on reaching out to the community and on loving lost people, they might not get their own needs met.

This led to some fascinating conversations about what believers have and what lost people do not have. Early on, whenever I had these conversations, I found that I lacked maturity and grace. I got frustrated easily. But as time passed, God helped me to respond better to the concerns of church members who were afraid of change. Instead of focusing on their selfishness, I asked them questions and then prayed that the Spirit would soften their hearts.

When people complained to me about our outreach efforts, about the financial costs, or about the changes we were making at the church, I asked them, "As followers of Jesus, what do we have that can never be taken away?" Sometimes the person stared at me with a confused look. So I clarified what I was asking until they understood. They often began to list elements of their heavenly inheritance.[6]

"We have heaven as our home."

"We have the family of God, the church."

"We have the love and grace of Jesus, the fruit of the Spirit, the gifts of the Spirit, cleansing from our sins."

Once they got rolling, they ended up with a great list of the heavenly storehouse of blessings Jesus' followers have. After conversing about all of that, I would ask them another question: "What do lost people have that will last forever?"

Very quickly, most people ended up saying, "Nothing." Or they said, "Eternal separation from God." Most of the time, this became a sacred and sober moment, sometimes accompanied by tears, as we talked about how people who are without Jesus, no matter what they might have in this world, really have nothing of eternal value.

From this point of biblical understanding, we usually began to have a meaningful discussion about how the church should use its time, resources, and influence to reach those who are spiritually poor. I would ask, "Do we really need to do more for those who are already in the family of God?" The truth is that most churches have all sorts of opportunities for believers to grow, fellowship, and be encouraged in their faith. The problem is that we don't really do all that much for those who are not followers of Jesus. We tend to lavish more and more on those who have everything of eternal value while forgetting those who have nothing.

We exist to love God. As Jesus taught us, loving God requires that we love our neighbors as we love ourselves.[7] When this love is alive and growing in our hearts, we willingly — and naturally — sacrifice for the sake of those who are not yet followers of the Savior.

ORGANIC GARDENING

PREPARING THE SOIL

1. What would your congregation say if you asked, "Do we believe, honor, and follow the teaching of the Bible?" What evidence do you see that would affirm or refute their answer?

2. What would your congregation say if you asked, "Do we love lost people and want them to enter a life-giving relationship with Jesus?" What evidence do you see that would affirm or refute their answer?

3. How much is your congregation willing to change, and what will they sacrifice for the sake of reaching out into your community with the good news of Jesus?

4. How do you respond to the statement, "The truth of God's Word will never change. Everything else is up for grabs"?

5. What sacrificial change has your congregation made for the sake of reaching out, and how has this affected your ministry to lost people?

6. What change or sacrifice does your church need to make so that you can take another step forward in your commitment to outreach?

SCATTERING SEEDS: HOLD THE BIBLE FIRMLY AND EVERYTHING ELSE LOOSELY

Lots of things the church believes and does are based on the clear teaching of the Bible. Other things we do because of tradition or preference. Make two lists of these very different things. In table 1, I have given an example to get the process started.

Biblical Absolutes	Tradition or Preference
Belief in Jesus as Savior	Style of music

table 1

Look at each list and reflect on what things are truly biblical absolutes. Discuss how we can be flexible regarding personal preferences.

SCATTERING SEEDS: COUNT THE COST

Study biblical passages that show Jesus being a model of sacrifice and selfless love, paying the price for us. List ways that Jesus paid the price to bring his love to the world.

- The incarnation (Matt. 1:20–23; John 1:1–4; Phil. 2:5–8)
- Washing feet (John 13:1–11)
- Loving and touching the broken and outcast (Matt. 8:1–3; 9:9–11)
- Going to the cross (Matt. 20:17–19; 27:32–56; John 19:17–37)

Study passages that call us to walk in Jesus' footsteps. List actions we can take that will propel us into a life of sacrificially following Jesus.

- Wash feet (John 13:12–17)
- Take up our crosses (Matt. 16:24–25)
- Lay down our lives (Matt. 16:24–25; Rom. 12:1)

WATERING WITH PRAYER

- Thank God for the truth and power of his Word, and pray for your congregation to hold to the teaching of the Scriptures with deep conviction.
- Ask the Holy Spirit to grow your congregation's love for the world and lost people.
- Pray for humble hearts among your leaders, longtime members, and congregants. Ask God to help the influencers in your church to be open to change and willing to sacrifice.
- Thank God specifically for the spiritual inheritance and blessings you have as a follower of Jesus.
- Pray for the people in your life whom you love who still do not know Jesus. Ask God to give direction as you seek to share Jesus' love and message with these people.

Chapter Three

Loving the Church

An Essential but Often Missing Piece

Most Christians realize that effective outreach is based on love for God and that it also means loving our community enough to sacrifice. What we often fail to recognize is that a joy-filled love for the church is also a key to outreach. If we don't love the church, why would our unbelieving friends love the Lord of the church?

As we have seen, the first step to helping a church prepare for fruitful organic outreach is making sure the heart of the congregation beats with a passion for God. This probably seems obvious. But many churches today are like the ancient church of Ephesus; they have forgotten their first love.1

A congregation must also love its community and be willing to make specific and consistent sacrifices for the sake of reaching out with the grace and message of Jesus. We must want people to enter a life-giving relationship with the Savior so much that we will give up things we enjoy and love.

There is still one more question we must dare to ask.

Do our church members love the church?

This might sound like a strange question. Maybe it's a question you have never asked or pondered.

Our answer to this question is critical.

A growing number of Christians today simply do not like the church. They are down on it. They have grown cynical. They declare, with boldness, their love for Jesus, but they are not so sure they like his bride, the church.

A PICTURE OF THE BRIDE

Picture the doors of a church sanctuary swinging slowly open. Music begins, a wedding march.

There she waits — the bride!

Every head turns.

The mother of the bride stands, and the congregation rises. There is a hush in the sanctuary as the procession begins. The bride walks down the aisle and every eye is fixed on her. Her flowing white train follows as she moves gracefully toward her groom.

Then, as the bride is halfway down the aisle, a woman points at her and whispers a bit too loudly, "Look at her shoes. They don't really work with that dress. What a poor choice."

Another guest says under his breath, "She's gained weight since the last time I saw her."

Yet another declares, just loudly enough for those nearby to hear, "Shameful! She should not have bothered to wear a white dress. Everyone knows her history. She and the groom have been living together for two years! Who does she think she's kidding?"

A man in the back shouts, "She's a whore!"

A woman leans into the aisle in front of the oncoming bride. "You're a tramp!"

Tension fills the air and tears well up in the bride's eyes. She stops. She is frozen, terrified. She looks around, expecting to find support, but instead sees anger in many people's eyes. She hears the whispers and insults growing. She wheels around and runs away. With tears streaming down her face, she sprints out of the church as fast as she can.

A DANGEROUS TREND

This might seem like a ridiculous scenario, something that would never happen.

But it did happen, and it does happen.

In fact, something like this takes place every day. I'm not saying I have ever seen this happen in an actual wedding ceremony. But what I see and hear is far worse, more hateful and hurtful.

Increasingly, members of Christ's own body slander, criticize, and malign his bride, the church. I hear the whispers, the backhanded comments, and witness firsthand some rotten fruit flying and hitting Jesus' bride. Some people even consider it hip to beat up on the church. Sadly, some of the harshest criticism, the most enthusiastic mudslinging, comes from those who claim to love Jesus and his people. Some Christian authors, people I respect, can't seem to write a book without including a few paragraphs, or even a chapter or two, that bash the church. Their criticism is razor sharp, and it deeply cuts Jesus' bride.

Just the other day, I was reading a new book by a dynamic and prophetic young leader who was careful to point out what a poor job the church does at calling people to real commitment and a life of radical sacrifice. Another author I respect had a bad experience in a hyperfundamentalist church as a boy and still makes a point of referencing this every chance he gets.

One afternoon at a gathering of church leaders, I had lunch with some of the speakers. I had never met the man sitting across from me, so I tried to engage him in conversation. After asking his name, I said, with genuine curiosity, "Tell me a little about your church context." He responded with harshness and anger, "I don't do church! I do community."

His friend, sitting to my right, began a conversation with him about how mean-spirited and harsh the church is. They both felt quite comfortable brutally critiquing the church in general, as well as specifying the flaws of particular ministries and leaders. I listened, surprised by their condemning spirit. They spent much of their time commiserating about how harshly each had been treated by the church.

One day, a song came on the radio when I was driving, and I heard some lyrics that pushed me over the edge. The song was about what Jesus is really like, at least according to the songwriter. In his estimation, if Jesus were to show up today, he would not visit one of our churches. I got the feeling that this singer-songwriter was confident Jesus would gladly and quickly go to the streets, the alleys, and the gutters of the world, but would have no interest in darkening the doorway of a single church on this planet. The message was beyond subtle: the church is a bad place filled with hypocritical and mean people. God does not like the church, and we should be suspicious of it.

I found myself arguing with the song and yelling at the radio, "No! No! No! You are wrong! Enough already! Can we stop bashing the church for just a moment and remember that she is Jesus' bride?"

As I drove, I thought to myself, "Jesus loves the church."

I'm sure he does.

Doesn't he?

A CLOSER LOOK

Don't get me wrong, I understand what this songwriter and most church critics are getting at. I know there is hypocrisy in the church. I am confident that Jesus loves those who are outcast, and I am certain he would visit people on the streets if he returned today. I know his bride is flawed. I am a pastor and I have seen the church's ugly underbelly. But she is still the beloved of Jesus. We can't forget that.

I have the joyful privilege of traveling around, ministering in different congregations and speaking to a wide assortment of believers. My interactions are almost always positive. I have broken bread with a beautiful group of leaders in a Lutheran church in the San Francisco area. I have preached the Word of God in a cutting-edge, arts-oriented Wesleyan church in Grand Rapids, Michigan. I have shared communion with a wonderfully diverse Reformed congregation in the Los Angeles area. I have taught a group of international leaders from the Church of God of Prophecy in Tennessee. I have spoken to a large group of Church of Christ leaders in Kentucky. I have preached to and trained leaders of evangelistic congregations in France, Switzerland, and the Netherlands. I have gathered for worship with passionate believers in Israel. I have sung songs of praise and celebrated God's joy-filled believers in Mexico. I have trained church leaders from an assortment of churches representing numerous denominations in New Zealand. I have spent the last two decades up close and personal with churches and leaders all over the world. On top of all of this, I have served as a church pastor both on the West Coast and in the Midwest.

In each of these places, I have encountered people who have enthusiastic faith, love for one other, hearts hungry for worship, and a desire to reach out to the world with Jesus' grace. In all of these locations, I have consistently been struck by the sense that God is present and that the people in the body of Christ are, for the most part, kind, sincere, faithful, and loving.

I've yet to encounter the judgmental, unloving, hate-filled, apathetic, and closed-minded caricature of the church that I have read about in many books and heard about from some ranting Christian speakers.

In vivid contrast, it was a breath of fresh air to finally read a book that called into question some of the negative stereotypes of the church, a book called *Christians Are Hate-Filled Hypocrites ... and Other Lies You've Been Told*.[2] I highly recommend it.

I am not claiming that all congregations, denominational groups, or ecumenical gatherings of Christians are perfect. Every church has its problems and challenges. But I believe that the church is still the beautiful and mysterious bride of Christ. I am confident that our Savior sees the church as it really is, warts and all, and yet still loves his bride. I am growing more convinced, as the years pass, that the church is far more beautiful and wonderful than we know.

If people decide they want to be critical, it doesn't take much effort to dig up some dirt on the church. But there are appropriate times for speaking prophetically and powerfully into the life of the church, calling Christ's body to new levels of devotion, service, sacrifice, and justice. But I believe much of our in-house mudslinging and incessant criticism has become almost recreational, and it breaks the heart of Jesus.

Our tendency to attack the church betrays an errant ecclesiology. When we beat up on the church, we aren't just attacking a faceless organization. We are criticizing real people. Some cast aspersions on the church as if it were an impersonal force, a pseudopolitical entity. But if I read the Bible correctly, the church is the gathered body of God's people. The church is an organism made up of people like you and me, the followers of Jesus.[3]

When we bash the church, we bash God's people. When we throw rotten fruit at the church, we are throwing it at our own brothers and sisters in Christ.

When we criticize the church and sling mud at Christ's bride, our vision for outreach grows hazy. It's difficult to invite people to meet Jesus and become part of his family when we can't stand his bride. How can we honestly want to connect spiritual seekers to a faith family that we don't particularly like? When people become critics of the church and slander the bride of Jesus, why should we expect lost people to be drawn to the Lord of the church?

If we want to see congregations become effective in reaching out to lost people, we need to help the church learn to love God, its community, and also itself. The days of church bashing and constant criticism need to come to an end.

I LOVE THE CHURCH

I was not born into the church.

I am an adopted child in the family of God.

When I became a follower of Jesus in my teenage years, Garden Grove Community Church became my home. People loved me there. They encouraged me. Someone gave me my first Bible. *Gave* it to me. It was a hardback Harper Study Bible, Revised Standard Version. Though I lost it years ago when I forgot that it was on the roof of my car and drove off, it is still one of the best gifts I have ever received.

These people prayed for me, kept me accountable as I muddled my way through my first steps of discipleship. They modeled a love and community I had never experienced before. They served each other (and me) in ways that made no sense. They were reckless with encouragement and enthusiastic with love. I saw Jesus in these people. I loved them, and they loved me. We were the church together.

When I moved to Wheaton, Illinois, in my college years, I discovered that the church was there too. It was a whole different group of people, but they also were seeking to love each other and to follow Jesus. Then when I moved to Glendora, California, and served a church for seven years, I had a similar experience. I have served as a pastor at a handful of churches and have interacted with members and leaders from thousands of churches.

Maybe I am blind or dense.

Possibly I am missing something.

Perhaps I have been hanging out with a select group of super-Christians who are gracious, humble, and really love Jesus.

But I don't think so.

I believe my experience is more the norm than the exception. I really do believe that most people who follow Jesus are seeking to love one another and to reach out to the world with God's grace. I am also confident that most congregations want to honor God, help believers grow up in the faith, and infuse God's love into their community. As I travel and meet believers around the world, and talk to those who travel far more widely than I do, I am encouraged and hopeful about the church.

I KNOW, PEOPLE IN THE CHURCH CAN BE MEAN

Please, don't paint me as a neophyte who naively believes that all churches are healthy and that every person in every congregation is saintly in all their behavior. I have been a pastor for more than two decades. I know better.

I have received my share of nasty letters. The worst was five pages long, handwritten, and two of the pages were devoted to criticizing my wife (who is one of the gentlest and most gracious people I know). It took every ounce of maturity within me, and lots of grace I did not have, to deal with that situation. I have faced my share of leadership challenges, power-hungry board members, and reminders of the power of sin in the human heart.

I have also talked with many Christians and church leaders who were hurt by a person or a group in their church who was not modeling the heart of Jesus. I know a pastor of a church-plant who was thrown out of the church he started. I have prayed with church leaders living on the ragged edge financially in a church filled with affluent people. We all have heard horrific stories of pastors and priests who used their position in the church to indulge in sexual sin.

The church, as the bride of Jesus, is made up of frail and broken people. There will always be darkness in the human soul and rebellion in the acts of people who name the name of Jesus. But Jesus still loves his bride, even with her warts and weirdness, and we should love her too. When we judge and condemn the church, we are attacking our brothers, our sisters, and ourselves.

When I was a seminary student, a wise pastor who mentored a number of us was fond of saying, "In the church you will always have the healthiest of people, the sickest of people, and everything in between." He would then look at us with eyes filled with compassion and add, "This is how it has always been, it is how it will always be, and it is how it should be. We are the church!"[4]

I will never forget those words. They put things into perspective for me. The church is filled with wonderful and loving people. It is also filled with broken, hurting, and mean-spirited people. It should not surprise us that being a part of the church hurts at times. After all, the church is made up of people! But the church is now, always has been, and always will be the mysterious, beautiful, and beloved bride of Jesus.

We are wise to remember this.

LOVING THE CHURCH

Rather than abandon congregations and expressions of the body of Christ around the world to start something new, and rather than become merciless critics who declare that we don't "do church," we must find a better way. The following are a few suggestions to guide our thinking about the church as the bride of Christ.

Develop a Biblical Ecclesiology

The church is not simply an institution or an organization. It is a living organism.[5] It is time for us to develop a biblical understanding of the church. We need to study Scripture and let it form our thinking. We should be discerning when we hear criticism about the church.

If You Are Called to Be a Prophetic Critic, Do It from within the Church

God will call people to speak hard truth into the life of the church. If this is a call on your life, do it with humility as a participant in the church, not as a detractor from the outside. If you don't love the church, you relinquish the right to speak words of correction. If you are not sure what balanced critique looks like, read the letters to the churches in the opening chapters of Revelation and learn from Jesus.[6] If you want to offer humble critique and ideas for improving the church, do it as one who attends, serves, gives to, and loves the local church.

Many of the critics of the church spend their time writing books and going from place to place to dispense their sharp-edged analysis. But they are no longer invested in a particular congregation. In some cases, they even speak about having a hard time finding *any* church they could attend. If we are going to love the church as Jesus does, we need to invest our lives in building friendships, serving side by side with others, and working through the challenges and experiencing the joys that come with being the gathered body of Christ.

Pray More, Criticize Less

I learned a valuable lesson from R. A. Torrey's classic book *The Power of Prayer and the Prayer of Power*: pray more, criticize less. Torrey calls Christians to be honest about the frailties they see in the church but then to pray about them: "If you don't like your pastor's sermons, pray until his sermons become great."

Criticism is easy to give, but prayer takes time and energy. Commit to pray more and to offer godly critique with a gentle heart. Before you unleash your next volley of insights on what is wrong with the church, get on your knees, cry out to the Lord of the church, and pray for eyes to see his bride the way he does. This might help shape your words and soften your tone.

Invite Nonbelievers to the Church

There are people today who say, "The last place I would ever invite a non-Christian to is a church." I disagree. What the human heart longs for most can be found in Jesus and among his people. It is in the church that we are loved, extended forgiveness, discipled, embraced, prayed for, and mentored in faith. The best place for those whose hearts are still far from God is among the people who have drunk deeply of grace and are ready to share it with others. That's what the church is all about. Of course, there are some unhealthy congregations that struggle to embrace new people and reach out. But there are countless wonderful bodies of believers who can't wait to welcome those who visit their fellowship.

Some years ago, I was called to a new place of ministry. It just so happened that my youngest son was at an age when he was ready to go off and find his own church. He had spent most of his life at the church where I had been a pastor, so finding a church was new territory to him. He visited a number of congregations in the community and had good things to say about each of them.

In one of the churches, a dear woman about four times my son's age reached out to him on his first visit. She let him know she would be his friend and help him in any way she could. He was delighted, and so were his dad and mom! It was refreshing to hear my son give a series of good reports about churches he visited.

I find my son's experience is more the norm than the exception. As you invite friends to your church, you might discover that people in your congregation are more welcoming than you think and warmer than you expected.

Look into a Mirror

You are the church, and so am I. The church's problems originate with sin in the hearts of people, including us. Before we take out our tweezers to remove the splinter in the eye of a brother or sister—well, you know what to do.[7]

If we spend undue amounts of energy critiquing and dismantling the church, it might be time for us to do a little self-examination. We can ask, "Am I greeting new people? Am I helping to create a loving and welcoming atmosphere? Am I giving sacrificially to support ministries that will bless longtime believers as well as the spiritually curious? Am I inviting people to connect in the church? Am I part of the problem, or committed to be part of the solution?"

When things get tough in the church (and they will), hang in there. Don't give up on the bride. Don't adopt an "I can meet with God just as well at home listening to a TV preacher or out in the woods enjoying nature" mentality. Although God can and will meet you anywhere, the Scriptures warn, "Let us not give up meeting together, as some are in the habit of doing, but let us encourage one another—and all the more as you see the Day approaching."[8] We should be committed to gathering regularly with God's people.

When Jesus looks at his church, he sees our weaknesses. But he also sees us as his bride, his beloved, beautiful one. It is not that Jesus ignores our follies, foibles, and flat-out rebellion. He knows us through and through. He sees it all. But he views us through the eyes of his grace and mercy.

The music begins.

The door opens.

In walks the bride, the church of Jesus Christ.

Jesus stands and watches her approaching. Can you see his face, the love in his eyes? Do you sense his passion and joy as she draws near?

Jesus loves his church, and we should love as Jesus loves.

For better, and for worse.

ORGANIC GARDENING

PREPARING THE SOIL

1. What are some subtle and overt ways people can beat up on the church, sling mud, and hurt the bride of Jesus?

2. What are some of the consequences of Christians spending too much time criticizing and attacking the church?

3. There are differences between criticizing the church and seeking to point out concerns in a way that will help the church grow healthier and stronger. What are these differences? What should it look like when we point out a concern to help the church become healthier and stronger?

4. I can guarantee you one thing: if you are part of a church, you will eventually be hurt by someone or something. The church is made up of people, and people can be harsh, insensitive, and mean. How can we love the church even when people in the church hurt us?

5. How have you encountered loving people, humble servants, and faithful saints of God in the church?

6. Why is it so important to remember that the church is people and not an impersonal institution?

7. How has the church been a family to you, and how has God carried you through tough times by using his church as a haven of care and support?

SCATTERING SEEDS: DEVELOP A BIBLICAL ECCLESIOLOGY

In the coming days, study some key passages in the beginning of the book of Acts and seek to get a clearer picture of what the Bible teaches about the church. Here are a few passages to get you started:

1:1–11	5:17–42	9:20–31
2:42–47	7:54–8:8	10:1–48
4:23–31	8:26–40	11:19–30
4:32–37	9:1–19	

SCATTERING SEEDS: THE 75 TO 25 PERCENT CHALLENGE

If you find yourself expressing concern about the church (in a healthy and godly way), seek to balance your expressions of concern with prayer. Spend at least 75 percent of your energy and time praying for God to move in your church, for the Spirit to guide your leaders, for humble hearts, for God-led change, and for all that Jesus wants to be unleashed in your church. Spend only 25 percent of your time and energy addressing concerns and issues.

Of course, there is no place for gossiping, complaining, and negativity. But if you spend thirty minutes talking with the right people, in the right way, about a concern, try spending ninety minutes asking God to bring health and life to your church.[9]

WATERING WITH PRAYER

- Ask God to help you see the church as he does, and pray for a heart that grows more in love with Jesus' bride with each passing day.
- Confess where you have hurt others in the church through insensitive words or thoughtless actions.
- Thank God for the many ways he has blessed your life through your being part of a congregation. Praise him for specific people who have become powerful conduits of his love and grace.

- Pray for people in the church who tend to be hurtful and mean. Ask God to help them experience a fresh work of the Spirit and to soften their hearts. (If you are in a group setting, don't use names or specific situations; just pray in general.)
- Pray that God will open your eyes to any way in which you might be bringing hurt to others in the body of Christ. Invite the Spirit to search your heart, convict you, and change you.

Part Two

THE MIND
OF YOUR
CONGREGATION

How does our thinking unleash evangelistic movement, or prevent such movement from happening? When our hearts are filled with love for God, for our community, and for the church, we are ready to strategize about outreach.

We need to use our minds to leverage every ounce of our intellectual ability for the sake of the gospel. Jesus himself told his followers, "I am sending you out like sheep among wolves. Therefore be as shrewd as snakes and as innocent as doves."[1] We are commanded to love God with all of our heart, soul, and strength, but we are also to love God with all of our mind.[2] Effective and world-changing outreach will not just happen spontaneously. It will take planning, strategic goal-setting, lots of prayer, and the effort of a congregation committed to sharing the good news of Jesus in creative and innovative ways.

Negative attitudes and ways of thinking can block evangelistic activity and prevent a church from taking the good news to its community. We can identify these attitudes and thought patterns and change them. Sometimes, just eradicating errant thinking will unleash the outreach potential of our church and move us in a positive new direction.

But there are also positive and healthy ways of thinking that will propel the members of our church into the community to share the gospel. We can align our thinking with Scripture and adjust our mindset so that we naturally follow where the Holy Spirit of God is moving.

In part 2 of this book, we will look at some strategies, shifts, and systems that any church can implement. Obviously, I cannot make a one hundred percent guarantee that every church will have the same results if they make these mental adjustments. Every church is unique and ministers in a distinct culture and location.

But if the heart of your church is already beating with a passion for the world, you should evaluate how you are strategically thinking about reaching your community with the gospel. As the Spirit stirs the hearts of people in your congregation, the mind of your church will need to be ready to think and dream in new ways.

Chapter Four

Seven Simple Mind Shifts That Unlock Outreach Potential

Our thinking shapes our actions. Sometimes a simple adjustment in our thinking can have far-reaching repercussions. If we shift the way we look at the world and the church, everything can change. And some of these new ways of thinking are far simpler than we realize.

Sometimes a very small movement can have huge repercussions. When a relatively little shift in the earth's crust occurs on a fault line, shock waves ripple for miles from the epicenter and can redefine the landscape. Changing how we think, even if it is a small change, can have a similar effect. Small shifts in our thinking can redefine the way we live.[1]

Throughout my childhood and teenage years, my family always had other people living in our home. Over the years, dozens of young people (mostly guys in their late teens and early twenties) stayed in our guest room upstairs. My parents never charged them rent or made them work for their keep; they just opened their hearts and home to people in need. One of the guys who stayed with us did something once that had a lasting impact on my life. It might seem strange at first, but stay with me awhile and I think you will see what I am talking about.

Eric, the young man staying with us at the time, came in one night after buying his dinner at Wendy's. He often bought a Frosty (a thick malt dessert) and placed it in the freezer, where it stayed until he finished his burger. I have never seen anyone eat as slowly as this guy did. Eric would take a bite of his burger and chew it for several minutes, really savoring it. Then he would wait, maybe a minute or two, before taking another bite. As a teenager, I could scarf down a whole burger and half an order of fries in the time it took Eric to enjoy a single bite.

After he was done eating, Eric would go to the freezer and take out his Frosty. He would slowly eat three or four small bites and then put it back into the freezer. His behavior seemed bizarre to me. Whenever I ordered a large Frosty, I would eat it right away, finishing it in a matter of minutes. Eric would leave the remainder of his small Frosty in the freezer until the next evening and then enjoy another few bites. He could nurse this kid-sized dessert for three or four days. The unusual thing was that he seemed to enjoy the few bites he had each evening far more than I enjoyed eating a large Frosty in one sitting.

I thought his eating habits were quite odd until I was older and began putting on some weight. As a young man, I could eat anything I wanted and somehow remain thin. But my bad eating habits eventually caught up with me. As I gained weight, I started changing my habits. I remembered Eric and his Frosty routine. For the first time, I realized that he had been thinking about the food he was eating in a radically different way than I had. I consumed large portions and ate quickly. Truthfully, I wasn't really enjoying my food. Eric ate slowly, and he ate less than me, but he savored every bite. As a result, he was far healthier than I was.

By my midforties, I was about fifty pounds overweight, and thinking about Eric compelled me to think differently about my relationship with food. I started slowing down at meals, eating less and enjoying my food more. Within ten months of making this small shift in my thinking, I had lost about forty pounds! My lifestyle and health significantly changed. It was all the result of a simple mind shift, a new way of thinking about food that changed my actions and transformed my health.

I've found that the same principle applies to the way we think about evangelism in our churches. A small shift in our thinking can lead to healthy ways of doing outreach.

In this chapter, we will look at a series of seven simple changes we can make in our thinking that can transform the direction and culture of our church. Just like the changes in my health when I began to think differently about eating, it will take time for us to see the results of these shifts, but the changes eventually will come.

1. FROM RANDOM TO STRATEGIC

In life, it's rare that good things happen spontaneously. Instead, we plan, pray, strive, and work, and *then* we see the results of our labors. The same is true in the church. Strong, thriving ministries don't just pop out of thin air. They always require preparation and planning and, behind the scenes, lots of effort and prayer.

If your church has a Sunday school program that helps children grow in their faith and learn the truth of God's Word, I can reasonably assume that you have a team of people who lead this ministry. You have devoted volunteers who study and prepare to teach classes. Someone writes or orders curriculum. You have a yearly commitment to recruiting teachers and helpers, to training, and even to a year-end celebration. By the close of a great year of Sunday school, hundreds, possibly thousands, of hours have gone into making this ministry effective in the lives of children, teens, and adults. No one would expect a church to have a powerful Sunday school program without putting effort into it.

This is true of any ministry in the church. Simply hoping that a ministry will spontaneously rise up and succeed is foolish.

We all know this. We understand the need to be strategic. We work to make sure that ministry happens where it matters most. But for some strange reason, many churches don't apply this wisdom to outreach. They just expect it to happen magically. Churches that fail to plan for evangelistic impact are, inexplicably, baffled when they don't see conversions.

> **Mind Shift 1:**
>
> We must approach outreach strategically and never haphazardly.

But that's exactly what a reasonable person would expect to happen. After all, we reap what we sow. If we don't plan for evangelism, it won't happen.

The truth is, effective outreach takes planning and work. In talking with pastors and leaders, I've learned that there are very few things that stall or disappear in a church more quickly than evangelism. I believe the reason is simple: the full force of hell is pressing against the work of outreach. Satan does not mind our potluck dinners. There are plenty of things our churches do that don't draw the attention of hell's minions. But when we venture into enemy territory to reach lost people with the good news of Jesus, the fight is on. We must approach outreach strategically and never haphazardly. Leaders in the church must declare, "We will think about outreach, plan for it, and weave evangelism into the fabric of our church life."

2. FROM FAMINE TO FUNDING

We also need to shift the way we think about funding outreach. Many churches will claim they have a high level of commitment to evangelism, but the vast majority of their budget is dedicated to serving and caring for those who already are believers in Jesus Christ. If we want to see evangelistic activity flowing from our church into our community and the world, we must fund outreach as a high-priority ministry and give sacrificially toward evangelism and missions.

I once talked with the outreach leader of a large influential church. This leader told me that his church listed outreach as one of their five priorities in their purpose statement and that the staff often referred to the outreach ministry as "the first among equals." When he said this, the words sounded great, but there was a cynical tone in his voice.

Curious, I asked him if he really thought his church treated outreach as the first among their five commitments.

He laughed.

"In our worship department, we have three full-time worship leaders and five support staff members," he said. "The church spends a huge amount of money on staffing for this area, and I think we should. Worship is one of our five areas of focus."

"So what's the problem?" I asked.

He took a deep breath. "I am the entire outreach staff for the church. And I am also responsible for young-adult programs and the church's sports ministry."

Even though the church publicly declared that outreach was the "first among equals" and a highly valued ministry, when it came to funding, the outreach ministry was given only enough money for one person to devote just one-third of his time to it. In contrast, the worship ministry of the church had a budget large enough to hire the equivalent of six full-time staff members. The outreach ministry was experiencing a famine of financial provision.

Another church I consulted for also said that they had a high level of devotion to outreach. But their budget told me another story. The annual budget was large enough to fund an entire worship department with multiple full-time worship leaders and support staff. But I found that the outreach ministry had no staff; it was led by volunteers. When I recommended that they consider adding someone on staff to give focused leadership to outreach, they made it clear that they just could not afford it. The desire was there, but the funding was not.

Don't get me wrong. I love great worship music and enjoy dynamic, Spirit-filled church services. I am simply suggesting that we need to fund the vision for outreach with the same commitment and passion that we fund the things that are designed to help us grow as members of God's family.

Let's be honest. Most people in our churches want great ministries that meet their needs. They want youth ministries for their kids and grandkids. They want inspiring worship. But when we talk about giving large sums of money to minister to people who are not part of our church, some people will push back. They just don't get it.

Try a simple test. Take a copy of your church budget and mark every item that represents ministry for those who are part of the church with bright yellow. Then, with an orange highlighter, mark items in your budget that are primarily for those who are not yet followers of Jesus. There is a good chance you will be looking at a page flooded with yellow ink.

Over my years of working with churches and studying the outreach strategies and budgets of congregations, I have found very few that give more than 10 percent of their budget to the ministry of outreach and missions. I've seen churches that wanted to dedicate a mere 5 percent of their budget to outreach receive strong resistance from church members who were worried that their needs wouldn't be met.

Mind Shift 2:
We must fund outreach as a high-priority.

When I accepted the call to serve as the pastor of a small country church several years ago, the church's annual budget was about $240,000. Ten years later, the amount budgeted annually just for outreach and missions was up to $250,000. During those ten years, hundreds of people had come to faith in Jesus Christ. Lives were changed, families were restored, marriages were healed, and countless seeds of faith were sown. As our budget grew, our commitment to fund outreach grew, and I am convinced that this was a key reason we saw our congregation motivated to share the good news in our community. To be clear: I am not saying God never would have reached these lost people if our church had not funded outreach. But it's unlikely that he would have used our church to do it. As Jesus said to his disciples, "Where your treasure is, there your heart will be also."[2] Our budget reveals something about our commitment to the work of outreach.

If your congregation wants to make an eternal impact on your community, it will need to make this mental shift: we need to fund outreach as a high-priority ministry. Never again can we let there be a famine of resources dedicated to reaching out with the gospel.

3. FROM BELIEVING TO BELONGING

Who is welcome in your church? What does it really mean to be a part of a congregation? In the past, it was assumed that people needed to cross the line of faith before they could be active in a church. Making a commitment to Christ had to precede the experience of belonging to the church community.

In the past several decades, our culture has shifted. Today, if we want to be effective in reaching out to people with the gospel, we often need to invite them to belong before they will come to believe the message we preach.

All around us people are looking for community, a place to develop significant and meaningful relationships with other people. They need to feel accepted before they will consider changing their beliefs. This is an important mind shift for many churches. We are more comfortable expecting people to adopt our beliefs and embrace our practices before they can be part of our church. But if we require this, many of those who visit our church will leave before they ever get a chance to hear the good news of Jesus and experience the love of God extended through his people.

Some years ago, a woman came up to me after one of our morning services, and she was angry! Not at me. She had been hurt by a friend, and she came to church because she was in pain. The Christian church and Jesus were not really part of her spiritual heritage, but she was curious. For about ten minutes, she shared her prayer request and used the f-word a number of times, quite loudly, as she told me about her pain and hurt. As she told her story, two thoughts ran through my mind. First, she really likes to use the f-word and has no idea that it might seem inappropriate to some of the people lingering in the worship center between services. Second, there is not a better place in all the world for this woman to be in the midst of her pain than in the church and among God's people.

After we prayed, she looked at me with firm conviction and said, "I like it here. I am coming back and bringing some of my friends." She was homeless and had a lot of friends. During the next year and a half, we met many of her friends, she joined a women's Bible study, she got in a growth group, and she became part of Shoreline Community Church. She did not come to faith for more than eighteen months, but she was loved, embraced, and part of the family.

I am convinced that this woman needed to belong before she was ready to believe. She needed to experience the community of faith before she was ready to experience the joy of following Christ. We did all we could to let her know she was welcome as she asked questions and developed a deepening relationship with members of our church family.

It can get complicated when a church decides to invite people to belong before they confess and believe in Christ. In this case, there were certain areas of service that this couple could not participate in until they became followers of Jesus. They were not able to serve in a leadership role, teach others, or have a direct spiritual influence on the children or students in our church. We had to use discernment and wisdom, but we found that they could serve in many other ways. They helped as greeters (they were warm and friendly people), they helped take care of infants in our nursery (with appropriate training and a background check, just like every other nursery volunteer), and they served in several other areas that our leadership deemed appropriate. We never gave them an ultimatum or set a deadline for how long they had before they were no longer welcome at our church.[3]

In many church traditions, people cannot become full-fledged members until they commit to Jesus. But they can still participate on many levels and be a part of the church community while they are investigating the Christian faith. I recognize, as I am sure you do, that allowing people to serve and participate at a deeper level before they have surrendered their lives to Jesus comes with some risks. I can't recommend a path that every church should follow on this journey.

What I can say is that, with wisdom and grace, any church can manage the challenges in a way that shows love to the spiritual seeker, grows the church's heart, and draws people closer to Jesus.

This simple shift in thinking has had a big impact on our church's outreach potential. We no longer require people to believe our doctrine and embrace our practices before they can be accepted in our church. Instead, we invite them to become part of the community as they wrestle with their questions about Jesus and about the teachings of the Bible.

> **Mind Shift 3:**
> We must no longer require people to believe our doctrine and embrace our practices before they can be accepted in our church.

4. FROM US TO THEM

"Pastor, what about us? Don't forget about us!"

I've heard these words (or some variation of them) almost every time I've tried to lead a church to reach out to its community. Whenever a church starts spending more than 5 percent of its annual budget on ministry to the community, it is inevitable; some people in the church will panic.

The problem is that far too many Christians believe the church exists first and foremost for them. They might not always say it, but deep inside they think the real purpose of the church is to meet their needs, provide services they like, take care of their families, and offer programs they enjoy. When a church begins to invest more of its time, energy, and money into reaching people outside of the church, watch out! An ugly, self-centered attitude can raise its head and roar at you.

When this happens, it can be a perfect time for a church to make a simple shift in their thinking. These opportunities are teachable moments for a church board or a pastor to help people learn that the church does not exist simply for *us* (those already in God's family);

it also exists for *them* (the people who still need to encounter Jesus' saving grace). This is an essential shift in thinking, a shift that can lead to big changes in the way people think about the ministries and programs of the church.

Those who feel threatened by the growth of ministries to people outside the church are not always motivated by selfishness. Frequently, I find that longtime church members have the sense that going out and looking for the one wandering sheep will take the focus away from tending the sheep that are already in the pen. They fear that the church will soon forget about those who love God but still need care, prayer, and encouragement.[4]

> **Mind Shift 4:**
> We must invest energy, time, and resources in serving those who are not yet part of our church family.

But growing believers and reaching your community are not diametrically opposed to each other. I have discovered through my years of leading churches and working with congregations that churches that commit to reaching out tend to have the happiest and most mature members, because reaching out to the community leads believers to grow and mature in their faith. And it gives them great joy as they see people coming to Christ.

Making a churchwide shift from *us* to *them* means choosing to invest energy, time, and resources in serving those who are not yet part of our church family.

5. FROM PROGRAMS TO PRAYING

The revival of Acts 2 was birthed through prayer.[5] Throughout history, prayer has always preceded great works of God. And today, if we desire to see a powerful in-breaking of the Holy Spirit and revival in our communities, prayer has to be the foundation.

You have probably figured out by now that I am not against strategies and programs. So why would I suggest that we need to move from programs to prayer? The sad truth is that many churches, when they finally decide to engage in outreach, jump right into establishing programs and forget to pray. I know how easy it is to attend a conference and learn about a new model or system of outreach and then try to unleash it on your church (and community) without first seeking God's wisdom, help, and direction. We often think that simply reading a book, buying a new curriculum, or discovering a fresh approach to outreach will automatically produce results.

Mind Shift 5:
We must seek God in prayer if we expect him to transform lives.

We should be thankful for great programs and new books, but we can't expect God to transform lives if we are not seeking him in prayer.[6] Prayer is crucial to outreach, and I challenge you to develop the practice of prayer in your church. At the end of this chapter, I have included some practical ideas for doing this.

6. FROM MUSH TO CLARITY

Theological clarity and a commitment to the teachings of Scripture are essential for effective outreach.[7] The doctrines taught in the Bible are the backbone of effective outreach. If a believer, a congregation, or a denomination compromises its commitment to sound doctrine, its evangelistic edge will quickly grow dull.

Certain biblical beliefs are essential to effective outreach. Here are four beliefs that your church must embrace with conviction:

1. God's love is revealed to us through Jesus' sacrificial, substitutionary death on the cross.
2. People are eternally lost without saving faith in Jesus and his work.
3. Salvation is found in Jesus and by his name alone.
4. Heaven and hell are real places, and real people will spend eternity in one or the other.

If a church grows soft on the core teachings of the Bible, doctrines that have been embraced by Christians for more than two millennia, it is inevitable that it will also soften in its conviction and desire to reach the lost.

I have found that the mushier the theology, the less passionate the outreach. Yet the opposite is also true. The clearer the theology and the more directly it aligns with the historic doctrines of the Christian faith and the teaching of God's Word, the stronger the committment to outreach.

Mind Shift 6:

We must move from theologically mushy beliefs to absolute confidence that God's Word is true.

Many leaders and churches fail to recognize this connection between core theological beliefs and outreach effectiveness. They hope that a great program or the commitment of resources and lots of goodwill and hard work will get the job done. But if the members of your church are not aware that people are truly lost without Jesus, outreach will not be a priority for them. Even worse, if the people who attend your church believe that everyone will one day end up in heaven or that Jesus is just one of many possible ways to salvation, they won't feel compelled to sacrifice their time and energy to share the gospel.

This mind shift may be the most important one your church ever makes. The doctrine of the necessity of the cross and our salvation through Jesus alone should be preached, taught, and rooted deeply in the soil of your church culture. Greater theological clarity and conviction will help you to significantly increase the outreach passion and potential of your church.

I once met with a church leader named Kyle Clausen, the director of operations and outreach leader at Daybreak Church in Grand Rapids, Michigan. Daybreak has solid biblical beliefs, but I've come to realize that even in good, Bible-believing churches, it's important to emphasize the basic doctrines of the faith. When I shared this mind shift with Kyle, he was skeptical and didn't think it was all that relevant to his church community. Still, he felt compelled to share the idea with the management team of his church at their next meeting. As he was explaining this concept, one of the directors interrupted Kyle to tell him that she was right in the middle of wrestling with the very issue he was talking about. She later shared the following testimony with the staff at Daybreak. Her testimony is a great reminder that we must not grow tired of teaching and contending for the truth of God's Word.

When Kyle began teaching in one of our meetings about a concept he was learning in his evangelism training with Kevin, I was on fire with passion! He was explaining the concept of people's beliefs and how they are allowing doctrine to slip and not holding it in high esteem. He talked about how some people are questioning the idea of a literal hell, being open to different ways of getting to God besides Jesus, and questioning God's judgment of man. He asked if we had experience with any of these things, because he had not personally encountered them. I want to share that I have had firsthand experience with each and every point that Kyle brought up that day! Over the course of this previous year, I have watched one of my family members change their entire belief system. This person grew up in a Christian home, went to Christian school, attended church faithfully, gave her life to Christ, and was baptized as an adult.

Then about a year ago, she innocently visited a different church and quickly spiraled into a place of biblical and theological confusion. She loved the church when she went because it was open to new ideas and thoughts. This can be a good thing, but a church should also provide answers. In this new church she was being taught to question everything but was not given clear biblical answers.

One thing that she began doing was finding out why people in other religions believed what they believed. She became so open to listening to what everyone else believed that she slowly, and unknowingly, slipped into embracing a lot of these things for herself. She had been swayed by a very charismatic preacher and by smooth-talking leaders. Her core beliefs were no longer based on the clear teaching of the Bible.

It has been both sad and scary to watch. She has begun talking openly with Buddhists and respects and encourages their beliefs.

I have been dumbfounded as I watch her question whether we are wise enough, as humans, to even claim to understand what the Bible means. She would argue, "We are not God, so how can we claim to know what he means in the Bible?" I have also seen her begin to question whether a loving God would judge people or if there is a literal hell.

I can only pray that she will once again see that we can whole-heartedly believe each and every word of the Bible and take it as God's complete and unwavering truth.[8]

Stories like this are being repeated in churches all around the world. We are facing the reality that churches today embrace unorthodox doctrines, have a weak grasp of theology, and cultivate a lack of confidence in the authority and truthfulness of the Bible. Leaders who are committed to developing a culture that reaches out to the community must preach and teach the core beliefs of the Christian faith and avoid the ever-present temptation to soften the distinctive teachings of Scripture.

7. FROM FATALISM TO FAITH

In the mid-1980s, I took a church-growth class at Fuller Seminary, and in the class, we discussed the challenges of turning around an older, declining church. The goal of our discussion was to think of fresh ways to share the love and message of Jesus.

The professor looked at each of us bright-eyed and optimistic seminary students, and he tried to give us a taste of the reality of church leadership. He presented us with a laundry list of the challenges we likely would face in trying to revive an existing church. He convincingly argued that it would take focused effort and momentum, as well as a powerful work of God, to help an older church move in a fresh, new direction.

I found it all a bit discouraging.

In the midst of his lecture, he used a line that is still locked in my mind more than two decades later. As he was talking about congregations that were not reaching out and growing, he stopped and with great emphasis declared, "It is easier to have a baby than to raise the dead!"

In other words, while having a baby is a common occurrence, raising someone from the dead is very rare.

And extremely difficult.

His point made a lot of sense, really. He was trying to convince us that it is far easier to start a new church than to turn an existing congregation around.

Still, that clever line never sat right with me. On a practical level, I knew that the majority of churches in the United States were in decline and were struggling to reach out effectively. But did this mean that all of us aspiring pastors should just go and plant new churches, abandoning the older, "dead" congregations? Did our wise professor really believe it was a waste of time to invest our lives in existing churches?

> **Mind Shift 7:**
> We must step forward in faith and not grow discouraged.

Since that time, I've come to see that there are several problems with this approach. First, having talked with many church-planting pastors, I know that planting a new church is very hard work. Anyone who thinks that church-planting is easy has never done it. The truth is, whether planting a new church or seeking to revive a declining congregation, a pastor will face challenges. Both callings require the power of God and the wisdom of the Spirit to succeed.

Second, I now wonder if my professor's words took into account the fact that Jesus is Lord over the church. I know that whatever challenges we may face in changing the heart and mind of an existing congregation, the God we serve is in the resurrection business. The same God who raised Jesus from the dead can empower leaders and congregations to move into a whole new season of ministry.

If we begin our work with a fatalistic attitude, we will inevitably grow discouraged. If we think change is impossible, we won't even try. But if we approach our calling with hope-filled faith and believe that God still raises the dead, we will commit ourselves to his work in our churches and expect great things for his glory.

As it turned out, after graduating from seminary, I was called to be a pastor at a small, struggling church. I quickly learned that God was there too, and over time the church began to grow and reach out. After several years, I was called to yet another small church that had never experienced much growth in its hundred-year history. The people, however, were far from discouraged and fatalistic. They were filled with faith and confidence that God wanted to do a new work in their midst, and he did!

God is able to do far more than we ever could ask or imagine, and he simply asks us to trust him and do what he calls us to do with hope-filled faith. We serve the God who raises the dead. It doesn't matter what the state of your church is today; God is ready to do a new work in your midst, and his Spirit is eager to breathe new life into your congregation as you follow Christ's call to reach the world with the gospel.

ORGANIC GARDENING

PREPARING THE SOIL

1. Which of these mind shifts would you like to see your church make, and what is one thing that can be done to help your church develop this change in thinking?
2. What is one shift discussed in this chapter that is actually an area of strength and healthiness in your church? What can you do to celebrate and keep growing in this way of thinking?
3. What can be done to help your church commit a growing percentage of its budget toward reaching out to people who still do not know God's amazing love and grace?
4. How can you help people feel that they belong and are welcome in your church community long before they embrace the gospel and enter a life-changing friendship with Jesus?
5. Why are solid doctrine and commitment to the Word of God so important for a church to be effective in doing organic outreach?

SCATTERING SEEDS: ASK A RADICALLY DIFFERENT QUESTION

The direction a church heads in often is determined by what question it asks when it plans its annual budget. Some churches ask, "What can we afford?" They plan the year's budget and ministry goals based on what they are confident they can pay for. This is what I call a faithless budgeting process. We never attempt more than what we know we can do, and we are never stretched or forced to trust God. When we take this approach, outreach rarely shows up on our radar, because outreach demands the presence and power of God.

But we can ask ourselves a radically different question: "What does God want to do through our church this year?" Once you identify what you believe God wants to do, you budget accordingly. This is what I call a faith-based budgeting process. When we ask what God wants to do, the answer always includes outreach. Jesus gave the Great Commission, and it remains the call for all believers today. I have watched as church boards asked themselves this question and then increased the outreach budget by 30 to 40 percent. And, by God's grace, the funds came in.

As a group, evaluate how your church plans the yearly budget. Is it a faith-based process? Try asking what God wants you to do and not focusing on what your church can afford.

SCATTERING SEEDS: CREATE A PRAYER CULTURE

Prayer should be a natural part of all that the church does. It should not be just a perfunctory exercise at the start and end of our gatherings. It is our communication with the God who loves us, the Spirit who leads us, and the Son of God who has saved us. Here are some simple ideas to help develop a culture of prayer in your church:

Impact Lists. The book Becoming a Contagious Christian by Bill Hybels and Mark Mittelberg gives direction for the prayer discipline of making an "impact list."[9] This is the simple practice of listing family, friends, acquaintances, neighbors, and others whom we care about who are not yet followers of Jesus Christ. Put this list in your purse or wallet, in your Bible, on a mirror, or somewhere else where you will see it every day and be reminded to pray for the people on the list. Pray for their hearts to grow soft. Ask the Holy Spirit to orchestrate opportunities to love and serve them. Cry out to God and ask him to touch their lives in ways that will open their hearts to his grace. Pray and pray and pray some more. Then, when a person comes to faith in Jesus, you will have the joy of taking them off the list, even as you add new people to it. Everyone in your church should have an impact list and pray through it regularly.

Prayer Walks. Train people to pray as they walk or drive around their neighborhoods, workplaces, and communities. You might even want to have people go out in pairs or clusters of three or four to pray for the community. As they pray out loud and agree together, your community will be impacted. (To the casual observer, they will look like people out walking and having a conversation with each other.) They can pray for the spreading of the gospel, for walls of resistance to come crumbling down, for God's blessing on their community, for the work of the church, and for people to enter a life-saving relationship with Jesus.

Leadership Prayers. Whenever you have leaders gathered together, pray together for the ministry of outreach. Allow time for board members to tell about people they are seeking to reach with God's love, and pray for them. When the people who lead your children's ministry gather, be sure they make time to talk about the kids who are close to receiving salvation and to pray for the children and the teachers. When youth teachers and volunteers gather, have them pray for your schools and for kids who are still far from God. Prayer for the outreach ministry of the church and for specific people should be a normal practice when your leaders gather.

WATERING WITH PRAYER

- Ask God to help your church set strategies for outreach in the coming twelve months. Pray that you will not be a church that simply hopes outreach will happen. (Throughout the rest of this book, you will find tools for leading a church forward in outreach. Encourage all of the leaders who influence the direction of your church to read these chapters.)

- Pray that your church will grow in its commitment to outreach and will invest more and more of its resources in the work of fulfilling the Great Commission.
- Confess missed opportunities to embrace new people and let them know they are welcome. Pray that nonbelievers will know they belong, no matter how long their journey takes.
- Ask God to help your church stand with confidence on his holy Word. Pray that your church's doctrine will be biblical to the core and not be shaped by cultural trends.
- Pray for your church to be hope-filled and confident that outreach is possible. Pray for faith in God that breaks barriers and raises the dead. Ask God to fill your church with a fresh confidence in what he wants to do through your congregation.

Chapter Five

Beyond Pushpins and Committees to Organic Outreach

Some churches support missions with prayers and money. Other churches take things a step farther and form a committee for local outreach. This is a good step forward, but there is more to be done. Churches that want to be organic in their outreach efforts will discover that evangelistic passion and action must permeate the culture of every ministry in the church.

Corinth Reformed Church had been doing outreach for a century before I became their pastor. They had a heart for people who are far from Jesus, and they were committed to the work of world missions. They supported missionaries, sponsored local ministries, and did a great job welcoming visitors to the church.

When I became their pastor, we committed to going even deeper to reach out with God's love and the life-saving message of Jesus. We soon discovered that the church's outreach ministry and its vision for reaching people with the gospel were limited and needed significant expansion. Over the next decade, the church went through an outreach renaissance, a three-stage movement that pressed us closer to the heart of God and drove us deeper into the world with the good news of Jesus. The stages of outreach development at Corinth progressed from "push-pin" missions to a more natural and holistic approach to evangelism, what I call "organic outreach" (fig. 1).

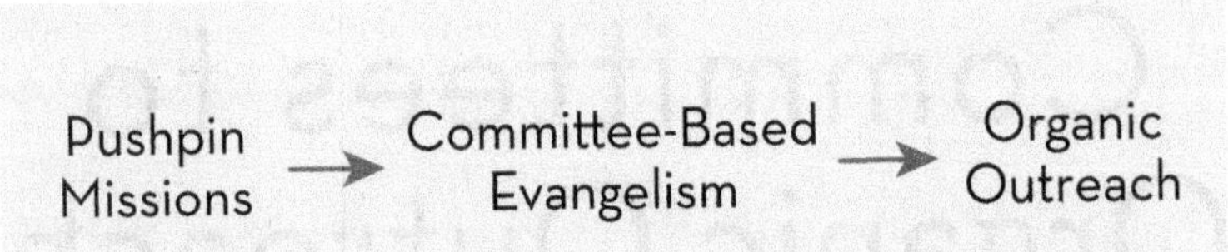

Pushpin Missions → Committee-Based Evangelism → Organic Outreach

figure 1

Each stage was progressive, built on the work that had already been done. As the church progressed through each stage, we bore even greater fruit for the kingdom of God. After more than a decade of developing a vision for organic outreach, we began seeing more and more people embrace Jesus as Savior and walk with him as the leader of their lives.

PUSHPIN MISSIONS

You may have seen it in the foyer, narthex, or lobby of the church—a map of the world with pins, flags, or lights indicating a country where the church supports a missionary. This visual aid reminds people that the ministry of the church is global. They are helping to take the good news of Jesus to the ends of the earth.

Displays like this can be helpful as an ever-present reminder that the world needs the truth and grace that only Jesus can offer. I love seeing these displays, and I am encouraged every time I find one at a church.

Congregations that have a pushpin display usually are engaged in missions in two ways. First, they give money. If you review their annual budget, you will usually find a line item that corresponds to each pin on the map, indicating a missionary or mission organization they support financially. The church has committed to give a portion of their resources to sponsor missionaries to go to the ends of the earth with the good news of Jesus.

Second, each pin represents a place where congregations send their prayers. In most cases, churches build a prayer network to make church members aware of the names and needs of "their missionaries," and the church lifts these missionaries up during worship services and in members' personal times of prayer.

Some congregations even communicate with their missionaries by email or regular phone calls, and with gifts at Christmas and on special occasions. These prayers and connections are a blessing and an encouragement to those serving faithfully all around the world.

We should applaud churches that support world missions. If your church has not engaged in this aspect of outreach, I heartily encourage you to begin as soon as possible.

But if your church is engaged in sending prayers and money to missionaries in far places as the primary way you engage in outreach, you should hear a few words of warning.

Pushpin missions should never be seen as the beginning and the end of an outreach ministry. A church can adopt an errant mindset that thinks, "We give to missions, so we have done our part to fulfill the Great Commission." The call to reach out to the very ends of the earth can include supporting missionaries, but it also means sharing the gospel with the people who live next door to us. For some followers of Jesus, the acts of giving money and saying a few prayers are excuses never to personally engage in outreach. Writing a check can assuage our guilty consciences, justifying our failure to share the good news of Jesus with neighbors, family members, or coworkers.

But when we act and think in this way, we rob ourselves of one of the greatest opportunities that God gives us to share in his work, and we miss an important and essential part of God's call on our lives.

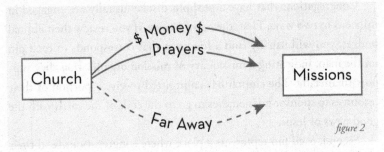

figure 2

So let me first say to churches that support the work of world missions, keep it up! The need to spread the gospel in the far places of our world continues today. Your gifts, prayers, emails, and encouragement are needed more than ever, and they can make an eternal difference. Let's never stop supporting those who have the glorious calling to reach out at the ends of the earth.

But let's not stop there.

At Corinth Church, we continued to support our missionaries with money and prayers, but we also made a few strategic adjustments that increased our effectiveness in this area. We set a goal to have fewer pins on the map but greater effectiveness in our mission partnerships.

You see, the pushpin approach to outreach tempts us to give a little money to a lot of missionaries. We stretch our dollars as far as they will go so we can have more pins on our map. After all, doesn't it look better when we have dozens of brightly colored pins all over the globe? But is this really the most effective way to steward our resources? If we are giving only a few hundred dollars a year to thirty or forty missionaries, are we really engaging in the work they are doing? Are we really making a strategic impact for the kingdom of God?

More pins on our map may look good, but it isn't necessarily the best way to serve those on the front lines of the mission field. Imagine what might happen if the same church committed five or ten thousand dollars a year to support two missionaries, instead of sending a small support check to thirty or forty.

I know, I know, your map will not look as impressive with only two pins on it. But let me assure you that what you sacrifice in breadth, you more than make up for in depth.

Consider the impact this can have on your church and the missionaries you support. Your church members can actually get to know a couple of missionary families well. Your congregation will have a deeper sense of being connected to them, and you might even plan a trip to visit and encourage the smaller number of missionaries you support. Your missionaries will be blessed by this change as well. Missionaries who are supported by small gifts from fifty different churches end up running from church to church when they finally get a furlough or a sabbatical. Rather than being refreshed, they are exhausted by the effort of visiting so many churches. Missionaries who are supported by a handful of churches giving larger gifts can travel less while on furlough. They can make longer visits and build more substantial relationships with the people in their supporting churches.

When Corinth Church made the shift to supporting fewer missionaries, it was hard, at first, to drop some of our missionaries and remove their pins from the map. But the results were amazing. As relationships with our missionaries deepened and the congregation connected more substantially with what they were doing, our giving to international outreach actually increased.

World missions should be in the budget and on the heart of every congregation. We should be strategic and shape these ministries to give strong support as well as a sense of connectedness to the local church. We can make sure each missionary is truly doing the work of the gospel and is sharing the saving message of Jesus. Let's never neglect the call to take the gospel to the ends of the earth.

But there is more to outreach than supporting missionaries.

COMMITTEE-BASED EVANGELISM

At Corinth Church, after strategically shifting our missionary focus, we also shifted our local outreach strategy. We did not stop supporting missions, but we added an emphasis on inviting people to be part of the work of outreach in our community. In addition to supporting missionaries around the world, we formed a second outreach team that was commissioned to mobilize our congregation to reach out right where

God had placed them — to their neighbors, friends, fellow students, and coworkers. We gathered about a dozen people who had a heart for the lost and gave them a budget and two primary responsibilities:

1. Plan *outreach events* to mobilize our church people to reach our community.
2. Plan *training opportunities* for church members to be equipped for personal outreach.

The committee got right to work planning and training. They did all they could to light the evangelistic fire in our church. And they had a fair amount of success. This team moved us farther down the road than we had ever been before.

Some people found this new strategy a bit uncomfortable at first.

"We send money and prayers. Isn't that enough?"

Our answer was a gentle no.

"Do you really expect *all* of us to be part of the church's outreach efforts?"

Our answer was an enthusiastic, "Yes! And we will help you do it!"

Our new team was made up primarily of people who had a heart for evangelism, people who wanted to see our church make a growing impact in our neighborhood and community. They began planning events, offering training, and doing all they could to raise the value of outreach in the church. More people were being equipped to share their faith, numerous outreach ministries popped up, and people entered into a saving relationship with Jesus.

For the next several years, our primary strategy for churchwide evangelism was this committee-based approach. Every year, the evangelism committee introduced two or three new ideas for outreach while maintaining those from previous years that were still bearing fruit. They mobilized volunteers to lead these ministries. They pulled in the youth ministry, the women's ministry, the men's groups, the children's team, and various other ministries of the church. They invited everyone to be part of the events they held and the training sessions they planned. Eventually, we had a brochure listing more than twenty-five outreach ministries that people could participate in, as well as yearly training in a variety of different evangelistic approaches (including the Becoming a Contagious Christian course, Sharing Jesus without Fear, Relational Evangelism, and several original programs we developed at the church). Over the years, as more people came to know Jesus, the church grew to about a thousand people. At the end of each year, we looked back and discovered that about 35 to 40 percent of the new people in the church had made a first-time commitment to Jesus through the outreach of the church.

It was an amazing, exciting season of ministry.

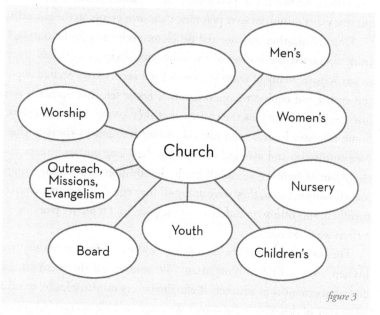

figure 3

Figure 3 illustrates the basic idea of committee-based outreach. You will notice that outreach, missions, and evangelism became an important ministry of our church during this season. In addition to our women's ministry team, our men's ministry team, and our children's ministry team, we also had an outreach team. We knew that it was important to have a good nursery program, strong worship services, and effective outreach, so we provided each area with a budget and developed key leaders in all of these areas. Outreach became one of the most valued and important ministries of the church.

But it was still just one ministry among many.

DISCOVERING THE MISSING PIECE

Our outreach team planned great events, developed wonderful programs, and held some excellent training sessions for the congregation. They worked hard. They learned that it took a lot of advertising, communicating, encouraging—even some begging and pleading—to get many of our people to come to outreach events. There was always a sense that our events were competing with the other ministries of the church. Sometimes, we planned a special event for the whole church only to find out that other ministries were planning their own events on the same day.

Communication was not the problem; even though the outreach team contacted the leaders of the other ministries and invited them to participate, many of these leaders did not seem overly excited about the events and equipping opportunities. Some felt that outreach was just another ministry in the church that they could choose to ignore. Some ministry leaders even saw the outreach events as rivals to their own ministries and avoided them altogether. The outreach team felt the strain of fighting an uphill battle. In addition to planning events and training sessions, they were doing all they could to convince church members and ministry leaders to participate, and it wasn't working as well as we had hoped.

For one of our churchwide outreach events to the community, we invited a top Christian comedian. We announced the event to the church six months in advance. We invited every ministry leader to take advantage of this wonderful event. We promoted it like crazy! Our outreach team felt it was a perfect event for our youth, children, men, and women—for every group in the church. The outreach team was confident that all of the ministry leaders would get on board and make this event a powerful evangelistic connection with our community.

Then one of our student ministry groups planned an off-site activity for the night of the big event.

It blew my mind.

I was frustrated (to put it lightly).

Almost none of our youth came to the comedy outreach, and few of those who came used it as an opportunity to invite an unchurched friend. I later learned that two other ministries also planned events for the same night and never invited the people in their ministry to attend the comedy show. We provided a great opportunity for them, and they didn't use it.

I was baffled.

The outreach team was disappointed.

In the process of thinking through these problems, I learned a new way of doing outreach that would connect all the ministries of the church more naturally to the evangelistic opportunities we planned. Eventually, this became my consuming passion — finding a better way to do outreach, one that would mobilize the entire church for the work of the Great Commission.

As I talked with outreach leaders around the country, I learned that most of them were facing similar frustrations. They would offer quality training opportunities for equipping in outreach, and very few people would show up. They would plan outreach events, and their church members and ministry leaders would not participate in them. They would work hard and pray passionately for the culture of the church to change, but there was still a subtle resistance to outreach.

Then it hit me.

After hours of conversation with other outreach leaders and pastors, a new idea formed in my mind. As I cried out to God in prayer and sought the Holy Spirit for wisdom, something finally became clear to me.

The problem was not with the quality of the events or the training opportunities; it was that the leaders of our other church ministries saw outreach as the responsibility of our committee. Sometimes they jumped in and participated, but we discovered that they felt we were inviting them to participate in "our" events. We were planning the training times and telling them they were welcome to come, but they had no sense of ownership of the ministry of outreach. They were ready to give us a pat on the back and cheer us on, but evangelism was "our thing," not theirs.

The truth is that they had their own stuff to do. Our other ministry leaders saw their programs as their top priority. Supporting the outreach team's events came second or third on their list of priorities, if it was on their list at all. They saw themselves as primarily called to do their ministry, not outreach. If they had extra time or energy, they would gladly support outreach, but honestly, how often are people in a church ministry looking for more to do?

Can you see the problem?

Our committee structure had taken us leaps and bounds beyond the pushpin approach, but now it was getting in the way. We needed a different structure, a fresh approach that would help our church members—and ministry leaders—see outreach as an organic part of every ministry of the church.

It was time for something new.

ORGANIC OUTREACH

When we recognized that our committee-based approach to outreach wasn't working anymore, we clarified our vision and took steps to establish a new paradigm. We kept our strong focus on world missions and continued to send money, prayers, and people to various parts of the world. We also realized that though we still needed the outreach leadership team, the shape and focus of the team needed to change.

Until this point, our outreach team had been made up of various laypeople, volunteers from the congregation who had a passion for outreach or the gift of evangelism. This brought a lot of energy and excitement to our team, but it failed to draw in the entire congregation.

We saw that our influence over the church would always be limited if we involved only the people who felt called to or gifted for the ministry of outreach. We realized that our outreach team could not be just an assortment of people with a shared passion. We had to involve key influencers, the people who served as the primary leaders for every ministry of our church. Our outreach committee was transformed into an Outreach Influence Team, a group of people with the influence to set the direction for an entire church.

God formed a picture in my mind and birthed a dream in my heart. I saw a large table encircled by the people who were responsible for leading every ministry of the church. I was filled with confidence that if these leaders personally embraced the responsibility for outreach, they would infuse outreach into their unique areas of ministry, and it would change the culture of the church.

No longer would we have a disconnected group of people planning and leading the outreach of the church, begging the other ministries to come and participate. Instead, we would have all of the key influencers in the church leading the outreach charge in their personal lives, with their leadership teams, in their areas of ministry, and for the whole church.

This vision formed the heartbeat of what I came to call "organic outreach for churches," a natural way of developing an evangelistic culture in a congregation or ministry. And I've become convinced that this shift is the key to transforming a church into a dynamic center of evangelistic passion and outreach ministry.

Can you begin to see a new vision when you look at figure 4? Evangelism is no longer the domain of a separate committee or ministry team. Instead, it is the responsibility of every ministry in the church. Those who lead outreach have influence over the whole life of the church. When you plan a churchwide event, the leaders of all your ministries are already invested. They "own" the event.

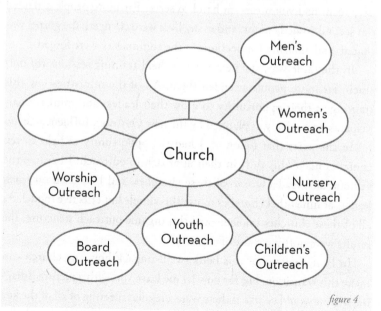

figure 4

Once we made this shift, things began to change.

The next year, we planned another big comedy event.[1] This time, it wasn't just a group of enthusiastic evangelists planning an event and begging other ministry leaders to support it. Now the group responsible for planning the event was our new Outreach Influence Team made up of the leader of our women's ministries, the head of our children's ministry, the chair of our church board, our lead pastor, the head of our finance team, our high school and junior high school leaders, the leader of our small groups ministry, and a half dozen other key influencers who led various church ministries. They were all committed to the event because they were personally responsible for planning and executing it. It was their idea.

As you may have already guessed, participation in this event was radically different from our first comedy outreach show. Every ministry was involved. It no longer felt like the outreach committee members were beating their heads against the wall trying to get other ministries to see the value of the event. A new commitment permeated the life of the church. No other events were scheduled for that night, and the whole church unified to reach the community through this event. Every ministry team had volunteers on hand to serve. Far more people attended our second comedy night, and many lives were changed, the gospel was shared, and amazing connections in the community were forged.

In the same way, the next time we held training sessions for outreach, far more people attended them. All of the ministries saw this training as their opportunity to grow their leaders and ministry participants because it was planned by the new Outreach Influence Team.

In the years that followed, I had the opportunity to help eleven churches make this shift in their approach to outreach. I became the key outreach leader at two of these churches, and I coached outreach leaders at nine other churches to use this simple but effective model. As all of these churches implemented this organic outreach structure, the results were nothing short of amazing!

In later chapters of this book, we'll unpack how any church can make this transition, but for now let me leave you with a picture. Imagine what it would be like if there were a regular meeting of all of the key influencers in your church for the sole purpose of advancing the vision of reaching lost souls with the gospel. Think about how this influence team could infuse new outreach passion and direction into your church!

You might find yourself wondering, "Is this really possible?" Let me assure you, it is more than possible; it is essential for the future of your church. And the good news is that God is ready to help you move forward.

I realize that you probably have many questions swirling through your mind:

- Who leads this team?
- Who should be on this team?
- What should this team actually do?
- Do our existing leaders and volunteers really have time for this?
- How often should this team meet?
- What should be on their agenda?
- How do you sustain outreach momentum in the midst of a busy church schedule?

Read on, my friend, for all of your questions will be answered.

ORGANIC GARDENING

PREPARING THE SOIL

1. How would you describe the outreach posture of your church right now: pushpin, committee based, or organic?
2. What needs to happen for your church to take a step forward in its outreach commitment?
3. If you are supporting missions and missionaries, do you need to become more strategic by supporting fewer people with greater resources and fostering a closer relationship between them and your church?
4. How might your outreach ministry change if all of your key ministry leaders formed an Outreach Influence Team and planned all of your outreach events and training?

SCATTERING SEEDS: FORM YOUR OUTREACH INFLUENCE TEAM

One big question the churches I led and coached in the area of outreach frequently asked is, "Who should be on the Outreach Influence Team?" My answer was always the same: "The people who can impact every significant ministry of your church." For some churches, this might be six or seven people. I have also led teams as large as twenty-one people.

Use the space that follows to list names of possible team members. Some churches will not have many of these influencers or ministries. Others will need to add some in the blank spaces provided. The people you list do not need to have the gift of evangelism. As a matter of fact, most will not. The key is to identify the leader who has the greatest influence on each ministry:

Key Influencers

Lead pastor:

Executive pastor:

Head of the church board, elders, or leadership team:

Head of the deacons or the finance team:

Small group leader:

Nursery leader:

Children's ministry leader:

Junior high leader:

High school leader:

College leader:

Worship leader:

Men's ministry leader:

Women's ministry leader:

Family ministry leader:

Missions leader:

Multisite leader:

Communications leader:

Technical leader:

Connections leader:

Facilities leader:

Recovery ministry leader:

Singles leader:

Other:

Other:

Other:

Other:

Other:

Note: You will be looking back at these names as you read the next two chapters, so it will be helpful if you begin working on this list before you move on.

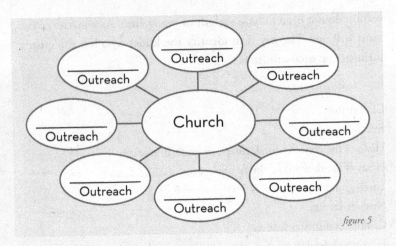

figure 5

SCATTERING SEEDS: CREATE YOUR CHURCH DIAGRAM

Use figure 5 (feeling free to add bubbles) to identify all of the core areas of ministry in your church. Note that outreach is in the middle of all of them. Don't worry if you have five bubbles filled in or twenty-five. Just be sure to identify every ministry area. To help as you do this exercise, refer to figure 4 on page 91.

Again, you will be looking back at this figure as you read the coming chapters, so it will be helpful if you complete this diagram before you read on.

WATERING WITH PRAYER

- Pray for your missionaries and that your church's commitment to world outreach will grow.
- Thank God for your church's past outreach efforts, and ask for God's blessing on those who have served faithfully in the past.
- Ask God to raise up the right person to lead your outreach efforts in the future.
- Ask the Spirit of God to give your church wisdom as it forms an Outreach Influence Team. Pray that each person who is asked to serve on this team will joyfully and humbly accept the call.
- Thank God for inviting your church into the glorious journey of following Jesus in his mission in your neighborhood and to the ends of the earth.

Chapter Six

The Six Levels of Influence

Mobilizing the Whole Church for Outreach

Outreach passion should flow naturally and freely from God into every level of your church ministry. From there, it should pour from your church into your community and the world. When there is a roadblock to vision and passion, we must identify it, overcome it, and get the outreach momentum moving again.

The heart of God beats for those who are lost.[1] He invites us into his passion for reaching people who are far from him.[2] If we are going to see the church become a powerful force for the gospel, it will take unleashing evangelistic passion, vision, and action at every level of our ministry.

It is not enough for a church to rely on a few zealous evangelists hitting the streets. Every follower of Jesus is called to be salt and light.[3] A vision for effective evangelism must permeate your church board, children's ministry, care ministry, youth group, worship music, preaching, custodial work, office team's attitude — it should affect every ministry of your church.

Organic outreach is a change in the culture of your entire church.

The apostle Paul wrote to his spiritual son in the faith, Timothy, "You then, my son, be strong in the grace that is in Christ Jesus. And the things you have heard me say in the presence of many witnesses entrust to reliable men who will also be qualified to teach others."[4] The word Paul has for Timothy is clear — pass on to others what you have learned. Make sure it is embraced by everyone in your church community. Paul also wrote about the importance of passing the truth from one generation to the next: "I have been reminded of your sincere faith, which first lived in your grandmother Lois and in your mother Eunice and, I am persuaded, now lives in you also. For this reason I remind you to fan into flame the gift of God, which is in you through the laying on of my hands."[5] What a beautiful picture of the message of faith being passed on from one generation to the next! God is honored when we take the truth that we know and move it to the next level, passing it on to others so more and more people can enter a life-saving relationship with God through faith in Jesus Christ.

UNDERSTANDING THE SIX LEVELS OF INFLUENCE

Passing the faith on takes many forms. Sometimes we pass it from one family member to the next. Sometimes an older person shares faith with someone younger. It happens in many different ways. God has a natural process for this to happen in a congregation. He wants to see a vision for outreach penetrate deep into the DNA of your church, and he rejoices when evangelistic activity becomes a normal part of a church's culture.

The following discussion of the Six Levels of Influence (table 2) will give you a big-picture perspective of outreach, showing how it always starts in the heart of God and ends up transforming the world. Each level is part of a progression, pushing deeper into the culture of the body of Christ and propelling the church into the world with the message of the gospel.

The Six Levels of Influence

Level 1 **God**	God is the initiator of all outreach. Organic outreach pours from the Father's loving heart, Jesus' sacrifice, and the Holy Spirit's seeking work. God's passion never wanes or wavers.
Level 2 **Outreach Influence Team Leader**	The Outreach Influence Team Leader is the person who is empowered to lead the evangelistic direction of your church. It can be your primary pastor or a person the pastor works closely with as a ministry partner. Every church needs a person who is a steward of the evangelistic fire.
Level 3 **Outreach Influence Team**	Each ministry of your church is led by one key leader. Someone heads up children's ministry, another leads the youth group, and so on. These people can be volunteers or staff. As a group, they form the Outreach Influence Team. They are the ones who take the vision for outreach to their areas of ministry.
Level 4 **Ministry Workers**	Ministry Workers are the volunteers and staff who are doing the day-to-day ministry in each area of your church, including youth sponsors, nursery caregivers, choir members, board members, small group leaders—anyone who serves in any way in a ministry of the church.
Level 5 **Ministry Participants**	Ministry Participants are all of the people who take part in any ministry of your church, including youth group students, women's Bible study participants, small group members, board members, office staff, and worshipers in your services. When they catch the vision for outreach, you know that powerful things are about to happen.
Level 6 **The World**	The goal of all outreach is to see the love of God and the gospel of Jesus transform our community and flow from our church to the ends of the earth. Once the church is infused with outreach passion, it naturally will flow into your community and the world.

table 2

Identifying these six levels is necessary to better understand how a congregation can infuse a passion for and the practice of outreach into every aspect of their church. As the vision for outreach flows from one level to the next, outreach becomes more than a program or temporary initiative; it becomes an organic movement. Whenever there is a roadblock at any level, the movement can come to a screeching halt. As you grow in your awareness of these levels of outreach influence, you will learn to identify where the roadblocks to evangelism are popping up in your church, and you will be able to make the necessary changes to move past them.

God's heart is for every follower of Jesus to participate in the work of the Great Commission. The Savior calls each of us, young and old, men and women, introverts and extroverts, new believers and longtime Christ-followers, to go and make disciples of all nations. The outreach vision of every church must go beyond programs and committees. This will take prayerful and practical imparting of vision and skills at every level of influence in your church. The six levels in this chapter will give you a simple pathway to follow as you make outreach a core value and practice throughout your church.

Level 1: God — the Source of Outreach Vision

Everything begins with the heart of God. Overflowing from the heart of God is an eternal, unchanging love among the persons of the Trinity. Jesus teaches us that God is continually seeking his lost and wandering sheep.[6] While we were lost in our sin and rebellion, God loved us and sought us out.[7] Jesus sacrificed his very life for the sake of broken and sinful people.[8] The Holy Spirit is the one who convicts us of sin and draws people to respond to the call of the Father.[9]

The God we worship — Father, Son, and Holy Spirit — is a God who reaches out. He is the primary seeker. If God had not initiated a rescue plan to save human beings from the consequences of their sin, if Jesus had not laid down his life and died in our place, if the Holy Spirit were not drawing people, no human activity or effort would make any difference.

Without God, there is no outreach.

The Father's love inspires our outreach. When we see God's desire to take the gospel to the ends of the earth, we are drawn into his vision and work. Because God is the one who initiates and leads all outreach, we can be confident that the fuel we need for the evangelistic fire to burn hot will never run out.

God empowers our outreach. After his resurrection and before his ascension to heaven, Jesus told his followers, "But you will receive power when the Holy Spirit comes on you; and you will be my witnesses in Jerusalem, and in all Judea and Samaria, and to the ends of the earth."[10] We don't have the power, in ourselves, for this calling. The Spirit in us brings power beyond description.

It is God who inspires, empowers, and then commissions us to take his good news to the world. God infuses his outreach activity into everything we do. He ignites the fire and keeps it burning.

Level 2: The Outreach Influence Team Leader – Someone Must Lead

Every church needs at least one person who will lead the charge for outreach. This can be the lead pastor or a person who partners closely with the lead pastor. Every believer in your church should be engaged in outreach, but someone must stand up and be the keeper of the vision. This is your Outreach Influence Team Leader. (Download a Sample Ministry Description for the Outreach Influence Team Leader at www .OrganicOutreach.org.)

I have been blessed to speak about outreach at many conferences throughout the years. Invariably after I speak, I am approached by a number of people who want to talk about their unique church situation. I am asked the same question over and over again. It is usually framed with caution and apprehension. It goes something like this: "I am the outreach leader at my church. I have a real love for what I do and a wonderful team of volunteers. But our lead pastor does not really support our outreach efforts."

I know what is coming next, but I wait for them to finish.

"Is it possible for us to have a dynamic and fruitful outreach ministry if our pastor does not support it?"

I usually say a quick and quiet prayer and then quote these words of

Jesus: "With man this is impossible, but with God all things are possible."[11] Then I tell them the honest truth.

"It might be possible, but you need to know that it will be very, very difficult." This is not a lack of faith on my part. It is an honest response based on interaction with many outreach leaders who do not have the support of their lead pastor. Normally, my response opens the door for a heartfelt conversation about the importance of leadership and the need to pray for the pastor's commitment to live and lead outreach.

I do believe all things are possible with God. I also know that when a lead pastor does not embrace the outreach vision, it is difficult for a church to move forward with a powerful evangelistic mission. When the pastor does not personally engage in evangelistic encounters with people, it is very difficult for the outreach leader to set a healthy direction for the congregation. The lead pastor's lack of involvement is a serious roadblock.

Some years ago, I met for lunch with a pastor who wanted to talk about how he could increase the outreach effectiveness of his church. He was concerned that they were not reaching out enough and wanted some fresh ideas. He asked me a series of questions about outreach programs and strategy, looking for ideas to mobilize his church members to greater evangelistic activity.

In the middle of our conversation, I sensed a prompting of the Holy Spirit. I hit the pause button on his questions and asked him what was burning in my heart: "How much time, in a normal week, do you spend interacting with people who are far from God?"

He was a little shocked. Then, he paused and looked down, saying nothing.

At first, I thought he was reflecting on the week, adding up the hours he had spent with friends, neighbors, and family members who were not yet followers of Jesus.

Finally, he looked up at me, made a circle with his thumb and pointer finger, held it up in the air, and said, "None."

We spent the rest of our lunch talking about the need for him to engage in personal outreach so that he could lead the church with integrity. He explained to me how busy he was, and I commiserated with him a bit, because I too live with all the demands of being a lead pastor.

We both agreed that our example as a leader is very important. If we are living and leading outreach, others naturally will follow.

If your lead pastor has a passion for outreach and makes time to engage with people who are spiritually lost, the pastor can choose to serve as the Outreach Influence Team Leader for your church. If your lead pastor's schedule does not allow time to take the lead in this ministry, your pastor can assign someone else to be the Outreach Influence Team Leader for the church. It is essential that this person works in close partnership with the lead pastor.

Can We Afford an Outreach Influence Team Leader?

Many churches struggle when they think about what it might cost to hire an Outreach Influence Team Leader. What church can actually afford this? Other churches might wonder why they should hire someone to lead this ministry when they already have a lead pastor.

If yours is a church that needs a person to partner with the lead pastor in this role, there is hope for you!

I was at an evangelism conference held by a large and influential church, and one of the speakers addressed the importance of having an outreach leader on the church staff. In one of the general addresses, he said, "Every church should have a full-time evangelism leader on staff. After hiring a lead pastor, the next and most important staff person is an outreach leader." I could feel the oxygen being sucked out of the room. I sensed that this pastor was a bit out of touch with an issue most churches face—a limited budget.

Later that same day, I did two breakout seminars with about four hundred people in attendance. I recalled the words of the leader from earlier in the day and asked, "How many of you have a full-time outreach leader at your church right now?" Only two people raised their hands. Then I asked, "How many of you see any possibility of hiring a full-time outreach leader on your staff in the next year?" Another four hands went up. It struck everyone in the room that less than 2 percent of the churches represented at a national evangelism conference could actually see hiring a full-time outreach leader. So what did that mean for the other 98 percent?

I encouraged them by saying that if they structured their outreach ministry organically, the role of an Outreach Influence Team Leader could be carried out with excellence in about five to eight hours in one month, eight to twelve hours in the next month, and ten to fifteen hours in the third month of each quarter. Personally, I believe this role can be accomplished by either a staff member or a volunteer. That's right, the entire outreach ministry of a church can be led by a volunteer dedicating, on average, less than twelve hours a month. It doesn't matter if you have a church of a hundred people or several thousand. The research and testing I have done over the years with the churches I have coached have proven it true, over and over again.

Who Can Serve in This Role?

The Outreach Influence Team Leader can be the primary pastor of the church, if this pastor has ten to twelve hours a month to invest in leading the outreach ministry. It can be another staff person who is gifted and has time to lead this ministry. It can also be a volunteer.

When I worked with eleven churches to implement the content of this book in different church settings, two of these churches had lead pastors who felt called to be the Outreach Influence Team Leader. One of these pastors was leading a small church-plant of around a hundred people. The other was the pastor of a church of about a thousand people. Both of them did an excellent job serving in this role.

In the other nine churches, the Outreach Team Leader was a partner with the lead pastor. Two of these Outreach Team Leaders were volunteers, and in seven of the churches, they were staff members. In case you are wondering, the two volunteer leaders did an absolutely amazing job.

If you have ever tried to start an outreach ministry in a church, you might be shaking your head right now and wondering if I have lost my mind. You may have seen a church invest thirty, forty, or fifty hours a week in outreach with limited results, and you probably think that eight to ten hours will never get the job done.

The power of the organic approach to outreach is that the momentum for the outreach movement does not depend on the Outreach Influence Team Leader. Rather, that responsibility rests on the Outreach Influence Team members, who serve at the third level of influence in your church. These are the people who lead all of your church ministries. The responsibility also rests on the Ministry Workers (the fourth level of influence) and on the Ministry Participants (the fifth level of influence). As the outreach vision spreads to each of these levels, hundreds and thousands of hours of evangelistic activity are released on a weekly basis.

The job of the Outreach Influence Team Leader is to fan the flames. This person does *not* lead the outreach programs or administer lots of events. The leader's role is to inspire and support the members of the Outreach Influence Team.

The Outreach Influence Team Leader also helps coordinate and support churchwide outreach events and programs, but this person does not have to lead them. Every outreach event or program should be "owned" or hosted by a specific ministry of your church and under the leadership of one of your Outreach Influence Team members.[12]

Outreach activity should never be led by a disconnected team that spends lots of energy trying to convince the other ministries of your church to participate. Instead, it must become the focus of every ministry in your church. When the Outreach Influence Team is functioning in a healthy manner, the Outreach Influence Team Leader is not burdened by running programs but is freed to inspire the team members and assist them in planning their events and programs.

Even if the lead pastor does not feel called to the role of Outreach Influence Team Leader, this person still needs to be a member of the Outreach Influence Team, and it is important that the lead pastor support the Outreach Influence Team Leader. The other key influencers in the church need to see the pastor following the direction of the Outreach Influence Team Leader and giving support to the team.

When I was called to be the Outreach Influence Team Leader at two different churches, both of the lead pastors at those churches became part of the Outreach Influence Team.[13] Neither of them had time to invest in leading the outreach movement at their churches. They both believed in the importance of outreach but asked me to take the role of the Outreach Influence Team Leader. With humble hearts, they followed my leadership. They were on the Outreach Influence Team of their churches and stood side by side with me the entire time I led the outreach ministry.

When I launched this model at Shoreline Community Church, where I serve as the lead pastor, I found a person who could take the position of Outreach Influence Team Leader and really move us forward. His name is Tom Green, and he started as a volunteer. Even when Tom was serving in his position as a volunteer, I placed myself under his leadership and clearly let the entire team know that Tom would be supporting and encouraging all of the team members — including me — with monthly infusions of outreach teaching, accountability, and support in our outreach ministry. When the leaders saw that I was following Tom, they willingly jumped in. I'm convinced that if I had refused to come to the team meetings and follow Tom's leadership, other staff members would have followed suit.

When I began training a group of Outreach Team Leaders from various churches around the Midwest, I told them that I would not even consider letting them into the "beta test group" unless their lead pastor was willing to follow their leadership and be deeply engaged in the process. There were a couple of churches that told me that their lead pastor did not have time to be on the Outreach Influence Team. I did not accept these churches into the program. The involvement of the lead pastor is not just important; it's essential.

At Lifezone Church in Tauranga, New Zealand, the Outreach Influence Team leader is Mary Opie. She is one of the most gifted leaders I have seen in this role. I had the privilege of watching her lead a full team meeting at a national conference in New Zealand. There were dozens of leaders from a variety of churches from the North and South Islands observing, and they were amazed. One of the things they observed was that the lead pastor of Lifezone Church, who also happens to be the national leader of Organic Outreach in New Zealand, was at the table, on the team, and fully engaged as a learner and follower!

Level 3: The Outreach Influence Team — Infusing the Vision

Hopefully, you were able to take some time at the end of the last chapter to fill in the bubble diagram of the key ministries of your church and to draft a list of names of people to serve on the Outreach Influence Team.

If so, you probably already have a sense of what this team would look like in your church setting.

Think of all of your church ministries (and don't forget easy to overlook ministries such as church boards, office workers, and nursery leaders). The Outreach Influence Team is the group of people who serve as the primary leaders of each of the key ministries of your church. This will have as many variations as there are churches. It is important at the outset that clear expectations be established of what this means to each ministry leader. There will be additional time required; it's not optional. This can be more challenging in a smaller church where most (or all) of the ministry leaders are volunteers. These people will be trained and encouraged and influenced by the Outreach Influence Team Leader on a monthly basis. Every month they will be engaged in inspiration, accountability, learning, and planning, specifically focused in the area of outreach (personal and ministry). They will be challenged to grow in their personal outreach and equipped to lead their ministries with evangelistic vision and action. In turn, they will influence the Ministry Workers they oversee. If Outreach Influence Team members are captured by the vision for outreach and live that vision out in their personal lives, it will affect the way they lead their ministries. There will be a fresh flow of evangelistic passion and fruitfulness throughout your church. Outreach will become organic.

However, if an Outreach Influence Team member refuses to take an evangelistic vision to their area of ministry, it presents a serious roadblock to the creation of an organic outreach culture at your church. I talked with an Outreach Influence Team Leader who was lamenting the fact that the youth ministry at the church was not bearing any evangelistic fruit. When I asked him if the youth leader (who was a member of the Outreach Influence Team) was committed to outreach in his life and ministry, I heard a painful story. The youth leader believed that it was his role to care for the Christian teenagers in the youth group. He had no interest in or commitment to reaching kids in the community.

Mystery solved!

No wonder they were not reaching any new kids. There was a roadblock at the third level of influence. This Outreach Influence Team member was refusing to let the evangelistic vision move into his area of ministry.

The Outreach Influence Team Leader really had only two options. He could work with the youth pastor to help him grow in his commitment to evangelism, which would require some willingness on the part of the youth leader to change his heart, his lifestyle, and his approach to ministry. Or he could remove him from his role as youth pastor, if he continued to refuse to be trained for outreach. This may sound like an extreme response, but the truth is that we cannot leave a person in leadership who acts as a roadblock to accomplishing God's purposes for our church.

During the time I worked with churches to establish an organic outreach culture in their congregations, I saw some Outreach Influence Team members experience amazing transformation as they humbled themselves, learned about reaching out to their communities, and began to lead in new and fruitful ways.

I also witnessed several situations in which a team member refused to embrace the call to be a part of the outreach vision of the church. In the cases where the influencer refused to change, that individual had to be removed from leadership in the church because they were standing in the way of God's plan for the church. Just think about it; God's plan is to take the amazing grace and good news of Jesus to the people in your community. If a leader is standing in the way, they have forfeited their ability to lead.

The apostle Paul said, "Follow my example, as I follow the example of Christ."[14] Leaders will be followed, and therefore they must be following Jesus. All of your Outreach Influence Team Leaders must be living an outreach-oriented life, even if doing so stretches them, so that they can help others to do the same.

You Can't Lead What You Won't Live

People have asked me, "Do you mean to say you actually try to motivate people to do something that is uncomfortable for them?" You'd better believe it! I do it all the time; it's called leadership. This is not manipulation or coercion; it is an effort to inspire, challenge, and hold people accountable to engage in the Great Commission.

"You do this even with your volunteers?"

Absolutely!

If a man or woman is not willing to commit to the Great Commission and live it out as well as lead it, they should not be in a key role of influence in the church, and they should not be on the Outreach Influence Team.

We need to reassert the priority of outreach as the central mission of the church.

Every follower of Jesus receives a spiritual gift or gifts at the point of conversion. These God-given endowments help Christians naturally do ministry that brings glory to God, strengthens the church, and often blesses the world. Some believers have the gift of evangelism, the Spirit-given ability to naturally share the love, grace, and message of Jesus with those who are spiritually disconnected. But we are all called to the ministry of outreach.

Every person who has received God's grace offered through the death and resurrection of Jesus should feel compelled to share this good news with others. Evangelism is the natural outflowing of a heart that has been transformed by the mercy of God. We are all called to love people and serve them in the name of Jesus. Every Christian is expected to be ready to articulate the hope and message of Jesus when the time is right.[15] We are to let God's light shine through us. We are the salt of the earth, and our presence in this world should cause people to thirst for the living water that only Jesus can offer.[16]

A fascinating reality I have seen unfold is that people without the gift of evangelism are often the best ones to call others toward a new commitment to outreach. Yes, people *without* the gift of evangelism. Since surveys tell us that about 95 percent of Christians feel they do not have the spiritual gift of evangelism, this should be encouraging news![17] Think of it this way: if Margaret is leading the women's ministry and she has the gift of evangelism, she will naturally encourage the women to take steps forward in that area. But as she does this, some of the women will probably dismiss her, saying, "That's just Margaret's thing. She has always been an evangelist and it comes so naturally to her. I could never do what she does." Other women without the gift of evangelism are inclined to dismiss her encouragement to evangelize and excuse their lack of involvement by telling themselves, "It's not my gift."

On the other hand, if Carol is involved in leading the women's ministry team and does not have the gift of evangelism but is still seeking to live out the call to reach out with God's love, that excuse is removed. Let's say Carol is calling the women's leadership team to engage in personal outreach and to plan a few outreach events for women in the coming year. She does not have the spiritual gift of evangelism, but she is living and leading outreach. Carol comes to the volunteer leadership team of the women's ministry and says, "All of you know that doing outreach is a real stretch for me. It makes me a bit nervous. But I know God wants to let his light shine through all of us. I also know there are many women in our community who need Jesus, and we are called to reach them. We should all be committed to seeing our women's ministry become a place that extends the grace of Jesus to the women in our community. God is growing me in the area of outreach, and I want to ask all of you to let the Lord stretch you too."

Carol's example has the power to influence others because of the fact that she does not have the gift of evangelism. A person who does not have the gift of evangelism can lead just as effectively as a person who does.

An Outreach Influence Team Member's Conversion Story

Craig grew up in a pastor's home. He went to church twice on Sunday and to midweek church classes faithfully through his entire childhood. Along the way, he felt a call to ministry. Craig uses his musical gifts to help people draw near to God in worship.

When I met him, Craig was a worship leader at Faith Reformed Church, a multisite church where he had been serving for several years. Not only had he been a worship leader, but he was being groomed to be part of the launching of the church's new site. In a few months, Craig would be leading worship in a town called Cedar Lake, a site that was intended to draw lots of disconnected people who had little or no church history. The heartbeat of Faith Reformed Church was clearly focused on outreach.

When Craig and I sat down to begin our coaching relationship,

I knew immediately that I was looking at a man with a deep love for Jesus, a passion for worship, and tremendous gifts for ministry. He was on the brand-new Outreach Influence Team at the church and was strategically placed to be one of the leaders at the new church site. I was serving as the Outreach Team Leader and was excited to invest in Craig and help him grow in his commitment to outreach.

As I cast a vision for how Craig might live and lead outreach, I could see discomfort in his eyes and tension on his face.

Eventually he spoke up.

Craig explained that he absolutely believed in evangelism. He expressed his support of my calling to lead the Outreach Influence Team. He even told me how, in the depths of his heart, he wanted to learn to be bolder in sharing his faith. He went on to explain, "The truth is, I have spent my whole life avoiding evangelism. It does not come naturally to me. It makes me nervous. I know it is important and I want to do it, but this really stretches me!"

I was blessed and blown away by his honesty.

As our conversation continued, I sensed that Craig wanted me to tell him what to do next. He was ready to give this whole outreach thing a try. I was sure that if I were to give him specific instructions about how to lead his worship team and the multisite movement on the Cedar Lake campus, he would follow them. If I had a program planned specifically for him, I believe he would have executed it exactly as I directed.

There was just one problem.

Organic outreach is not about a program or a plan. It's about orienting our hearts toward God and letting him lead us. It's about seeking the direction of the Holy Spirit. It's about being ever ready to respond when God opens a door.

I was not the person called to lead the worship ministry on the Cedar Lake campus of Faith Church. Craig was. So I told him, "You need to ask God how he wants you to live out the call to outreach in your new ministry setting. Then you need to seek the Spirit's leading for how you are to lead your team of musicians and technical people in their outreach on the Cedar Lake campus."

He looked at me a bit skeptically, but I assured him that God knew exactly what steps he needed to take. I reminded him that he was the one God had called to lead the worship ministry at the new campus, not me. He was the one best equipped to listen to God and lead the charge.

This is why someone serving as an Outreach Influence Team Leader can do their job in about eight to ten hours a week. The Outreach Influence Team Leader does not plan all of the programs, but he encourages and inspires the Outreach Influence Team members to seek God and design their own direction for outreach. The results are consistently surprising and glorious.

The next time we met, Craig told me that he had heard from God and knew just what the team needed to do. He explained that they would be practicing the music a little earlier than planned on their first Sunday. They would finish fifteen minutes before the start of the service so they had time to connect with visitors and people who were gathering for worship.

This was a new concept for the church. The main church campus has a comfortable room for the worship leaders to hang out in before services. Since there are four weekend services, this is a nice place for the musicians to take a break between services. Unfortunately, it can also keep them from engaging with the congregation, potentially blocking some wonderful outreach connections.[18]

Craig went on to tell me that he was nervous, but he felt this commitment would stretch him in a good way. He shared that when he first brought this idea to the musicians on his team, he was pretty sure they would resist the change. To his surprise, they loved the idea and jumped right on board.

When the Cedar Lake campus finally launched, Craig and his entire worship team walked across the stage to greet and connect with people. They enjoyed the time so much that when the music was supposed to begin, Craig had to drag the musicians out of the congregation and onto the stage. That first morning, they started a couple of minutes behind schedule because the musicians were engaged in conversations.

This is just one of many examples of how an Outreach Influence Team member can accept the challenge to engage in outreach on a personal level and lead it in their area of ministry. For Craig, though he had been converted to Jesus years before as a young boy, he was now being converted to living an outreach-oriented life and leading others in outreach.

Level 4: Ministry Workers — Faithful Servants in Every Area of the Church

The fourth level of outreach influence in the church is the Ministry Workers: all of those who serve in any type of ministry in a church. These are your nursery volunteers, those who help in the youth ministry, the women who lead the women's ministry, small group leaders, board members — anyone who serves in any way in a ministry of the church. Influencing outreach at this fourth level is a critical part of the organic outreach process.

When the Outreach Influence Team Leader senses the vision for outreach from the heart of God, they seek to instill it in the members of the Outreach Influence Team. With monthly training, accountability, and encouragement, these team members begin to live outreach in a new way. As they do this, they naturally take this vision to Ministry Workers in their specific areas of ministry. The high school leader takes a new vision for outreach to the youth volunteers he works with and trains. The women's ministry leader instills this passion for outreach in the women who lead small group Bible studies. The nursery leader helps all the volunteers in the nursery ministry understand how they are involved in outreach every time they care for children. The leader of the church board begins to do devotionals at the start of each meeting that challenge the other board members to enter into personal outreach and see the essential place of evangelism in the church.

Imagine a junior high ministry leader who has ten volunteers working with students. If these Ministry Workers are praying for their lost friends and reaching out to them, they will naturally encourage their junior high kids to do the same. That's what makes this form of outreach organic; it's more than a program.

Try to get this picture in your mind. If your church has about a hundred and twenty-five people, there are probably around fifty who are Ministry Workers. If they are being encouraged to engage in outreach, you won't be able to stop the evangelistic momentum.[19]

Level 5: Ministry Participants — Touching Every Part of Your Church

When the Outreach Influence Team members and the Ministry Workers who serve with them capture the vision for outreach, things really begin to heat up! Your key ministry leaders and workers are now praying and living an outreach-oriented lifestyle. Through their example and teaching, all of the Ministry Participants in their areas of ministry will also be encouraged to reach out and be part of God's plan for spreading the Good News.

When Ministry Participants step off the sidelines and finally get into the outreach game, you know things are about to change. When the youth pastor, a member of the Outreach Influence Team, gets the vision for outreach and starts influencing the Ministry Workers, it's not the end of the story. That youth pastor and those Ministry Workers begin inviting the students (Ministry Participants) to begin reaching out on their campuses, and the message of Jesus now moves naturally into schools, into neighborhoods, onto sports fields, and into homes all over your community. The good news of Jesus begins flowing from your church into your community and to the world.

When Ministry Participants catch the vision for outreach from those who minister to them and sense the call of God to reach out, they become a mighty force for the gospel, and the church becomes an outreach church. The process is organic. Natural. The church becomes what God longs for it to be.

Level 6: The World — Becoming Grace-Bearers

So where does all of this end? What is the final level of influence? We began in the heart of God (level 1), whose love and passion for the lost ignited the heart of an Outreach Influence Team Leader (level 2). This leader communicated the outreach vision to the Outreach Influence Team (level 3), a group made up of the key leaders and influencers in each ministry of your church. The Outreach Influence Team members, as they were challenged in their passion to reach out, naturally poured this vision into their areas of ministry, influencing the lives of their Ministry Workers (level 4). These Ministry Workers, as they followed the example of their leaders, instilled the passion for outreach in the hearts of those they minister to, the Ministry Participants (level 5). And now, your church is saturated with the outreach vision. The culture of your church community has changed. Everything you do as a church has an outreach focus. Church members receive regular reminders and training, and sharing the gospel is a natural part of their identity as followers of Christ.

Now your church is becoming what God intended it to be. Every day, passionate and committed people from your church are scattered all over your community and throughout the world. They love and serve lost people and share God's good news with them. Hundreds, maybe thousands, of people leave your church each weekend with a huge potential to impact their neighbors and friends.

The goal of organic outreach is realized when those who belong to your church begin sharing their story of faith naturally, throughout the week. People know they can invite nonbelieving friends to your church because it is an accepting and loving environment filled with people who care about those who are still far from God. The tide will shift when the majority of your church members begin praying faithfully for those who are lost and when they shed tears for the broken of this world who need the healing only Jesus can provide. Your church members begin to see themselves as missionaries right in their own community. They are now confident to share the message of Jesus and to serve in the name of the God who loves them.

Organic outreach is not a program, an outreach event, or a system. At the core, it's about people falling in love with Jesus and letting his heart transform their own. When all six levels of influence are engaged in this process of transformation, your church will overflow with the life-changing love of God.

LEVEL JUMPING

I was meeting with a group of Outreach Influence Team Leaders from a number of different churches. One of them candidly shared how the spread of the outreach vision in their church did not follow this six-step progression exactly as it is described in this chapter. In this case, one of the Outreach Influence Team members, the high school ministry leader in the church, was a roadblock to outreach. This ministry leader was fearful of evangelism and was not reaching out, much less leading others in how to reach out.

But God did something wonderful and beautiful.

Even though the high school ministry leader had resisted the outreach training and encouragement the Outreach Influence Team Leader was giving him, the high school students in the ministry began praying with new passion, reaching out to their friends and fellow students, and evangelizing! A revival began at the high school as students started leading their friends to Jesus. The Spirit of God showed up and began touching lives, even though the youth leader and his Ministry Workers were not leading what was happening.

In this case, the vision did not trickle down from the leaders and volunteers; it erupted in the lives of the students. God just showed up among them and began changing hearts. How cool is that?

In the coming months, there was actually a reversal of influence as the Ministry Workers began catching the vision from the students. Eventually, the youth pastor also caught the vision as his ministry volunteers were fired up from their interaction with the students they served. Outreach influence moved in the opposite direction in this case, from level 5 (Ministry Participants) to level 4 (Ministry Workers) to level 3 (Outreach Influence Team member).

Is this okay?

Should we encourage this?

Of course! God is God, and he will show up when and where he wants to accomplish his will in any way he sees fit.

I praise God when things don't go the way we plan, and I give thanks for this Spirit-empowered movement. The progression I've suggested in this chapter is just one approach, a reproducible pattern that often leads to the development of a fruitful outreach culture in a church. And in most cases, it will be the primary way of engaging people in the outreach vision. But if the Spirit plants seeds at different levels, don't be afraid to reap the harvest and give God the praise.

ORGANIC GARDENING

PREPARING THE SOIL

1. How does God's example as the level 1 "leader" in our outreach efforts inspire us?
2. How does the Father partner with us in this work? What has Jesus, the Son, done to make the gospel available to lost people? How is the Holy Spirit working to empower us in the ministry of outreach?
3. As you think about the role of an Outreach Influence Team Leader (level 2), the role of the Outreach Influence Team (level 3), and the various people involved as Ministry Workers in your church (level 4), how do you see God preparing the way for your congregation to move toward a more organic model of outreach?
4. What can be done to grow God's heart for outreach in every area of your church using the model of the Six Levels of Influence?

SCATTERING SEEDS: IDENTIFY ROADBLOCKS

Where in the Six Levels of Influence is the vision for outreach breaking down in your church? Where is it strong?

SCATTERING SEEDS: BEGIN AN OUTREACH INFLUENCE TEAM

The process of beginning an Outreach Influence Team should be led by your Outreach Influence Team Leader. This team should include all of the leaders of every ministry. Make a list of the people you believe should be on this team and begin praying for them.

SCATTERING SEEDS: TAKE A BLESSING

Encourage your Outreach Influence Team members as they seek to take an evangelistic vision to their areas of ministry. Celebrate when their ministries bear fruit, and cheer them on as they seek to grow the outreach emphasis right where they are called to lead.

WATERING WITH PRAYER

- Pray for God to raise up an Outreach Influence Team Leader if you do not have one at this time. Ask God to empower this leader and use his or her life as a tool to take the outreach vision into the leadership culture of your church. Ask God to give this leader passion, growing vision, and a lifestyle that engages in outreach. Pray also that they will fulfill their calling to help form an Outreach Influence Team as they go deeper in their calling to the ministry of outreach.
- Ask God to prepare each person who will become an Outreach Influence Team member. Ask God to give them teachable hearts. Pray that their passion for outreach and heart for the lost will grow. Ask the Holy Spirit to fill them with new power as they lead their ministries and seek to add a fresh new focus on outreach.
- Pray for all of the Ministry Workers in your church. Ask God to help them be open to a new emphasis on outreach in their ministries and personal lives. Ask God to use these faithful workers to impact the Ministry Participants they serve.
- Ask God to use your whole church, in fresh new ways, to impact your community with the gospel. Invite the Holy Spirit to fill your church to overflowing so that the love and message of Jesus will flow from your church to the ends of the earth.

Chapter Seven

Raising the Evangelistic Temperature

The One-Degree Rule

Every church has an outreach temperature. If a congregation wants to make evangelism an enduring central focus, it will strategically seek to raise the temperature of each leader and every ministry.

It's a cool fall evening, and you are outdoors with a fire blazing and crackling away. Friends are gathered around in lawn chairs sharing stories. Laughter and smoke from the fire waft toward the starry sky. It's one of those "Kumbaya" moments that we all treasure, a taste of heaven on earth.

As the evening presses on, the fire cools and fades. The embers glow as the night grows darker. The flames are gone, but there is still warmth. What was once a blazing campfire is now nothing but a pile of ashes and a few embers.

This is the way of fires. To keep burning, they need fuel.

When it comes to keeping our evangelistic fires burning, it's no different.

THE ONE-DEGREE RULE

Every follower of Jesus has an outreach temperature, whether it's hot, cold, or somewhere in the middle. This temperature impacts the way we live and interact with those who are far from God. It is our responsibility to increase this temperature so that our hearts burn hotter for those who are spiritually disconnected. The One-Degree Rule is a simple concept that can help followers of Jesus see their need to grow and then take a practical step to increase their passion to reach out.

I use a scale of one to ten to help identify where we are in our evangelistic passion. (See fig. 6.) In our individual lives, a ten represents a heart that is sizzling hot for evangelism.[1] When we are at a ten, we pray often, notice people who are spiritually wandering, and enjoy making time in our schedule to connect with those who are far from God. In these seasons, our lights are shining, we speak of our faith often, we share stories of what God is doing in our lives, and we share the gospel naturally.

When our personal temperature is at a one, our hearts have cooled off. We are no longer praying for lost people, and we have become too busy with church programs or our personal interests to make space for people who are outside of God's family. We walk right past opportunities to let the light of Jesus shine and hardly notice. We rarely tell others about our faith, and we do not feel much urgency to communicate the gospel of Jesus. We are ice cold.

In the same way, we can also identify the outreach temperature of our church ministries. In a church, an eight or a nine represents the times when a ministry is welcoming of those who are lost, when its members are praying for people to come to faith in Jesus, and when a ministry is designing its gatherings to attract those who are not yet in a

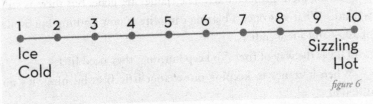

figure 6

saving relationship with Jesus. A ministry has a high outreach temperature when its leaders and workers are consistently seeing nonchurched visitors attend and when these spiritual seekers are hearing about the amazing love of God, are having meaningful spiritual conversations, and are entering a relationship with Jesus.

We know a ministry's temperature is low when its participants are content to get together with a bunch of other Christians to have fun. Our temperature is cooling off when we invest most of our energy in planning activities for those who are already in God's family. If we are not hearing stories of people coming to faith in Christ, and if the message of God's love is not being communicated regularly, our temperature is growing cold.

Over the years as I have used this simple tool, I have not found a single person who fails to grasp this concept. I can explain it to a small group leader, and after reflecting for a few seconds, he can tell me the temperature of his small group ministry: "I think our groups have become very closed and inwardly focused; our temperature is at a two." I can talk with a high school ministry leader, and she can say to me, "We are at an eight! We are really reaching out, and the spirit of our group is very inviting."

The value of the One-Degree Rule is that it doesn't matter what the starting number is. The purpose is to commit to raise that number by one degree. The real issue is not whether the women's ministry temperature is at a three or a seven; the One-Degree Rule begins a conversation about the steps needed to raise the temperature one degree higher. If the church board identifies the church's temperature as a seven, even if they have overestimated, they will still begin strategizing to raise it one degree. If the children's ministry temperature is a five, add some fuel and get them thinking about how to raise it to a six.

At this point, you might be asking, "What if our ministry temperature is at a ten?" If this is this case (which is very rare, in my experience), just make the top of your scale eleven and take things up another degree. The key to this simple concept is realizing that we can always turn the temperature up a bit higher. We can always add a little more fuel to the outreach fire burning in our ministry.

Over the years as I've trained Outreach Influence Team leaders and members, I have discovered that they always have a fairly accurate sense of their ministrys' outreach temperature. And they often can identify the action needed to stoke the fire and increase the outreach passion for each ministry. The problem isn't lack of awareness or ideas; it's taking the time to do something about it. The One-Degree Rule encourages each ministry team in your church to focus on outreach and to increase their ministry's passion and commitment. The result will be more passionate outreach to people who are far from God.

One of the best ways we can help believers grow in their commitment to outreach is to help them identify their personal evangelistic temperature and then seek to raise it by one degree. This can easily be done in a variety of ministry settings.

I recommend that every ministry team regularly tend their outreach fire. Each time the church board meets, they should talk about their personal outreach temperature, as well as the outreach temperature of the whole church. Every other ministry leadership team in your church should plan regular times to honestly discuss what their personal and ministry temperatures are and to identify ways to increase these temperatures by one degree. This will give you a simple but recurring way to tend the evangelistic fires in your church and make sure they are burning hot.

When we are attentive to our own temperature and focused on bringing it up a degree, we are more receptive to the opportunities God provides for us to share the message of Jesus and the grace he offers.

RAISING THE LEADERSHIP BAR

Imagine a church board or staff team gathered for their monthly meeting. They know that every single time they gather, someone will ask them, "What is your personal evangelism temperature?" Next, they are going to be asked, "What is the outreach temperature of our church?" Each person knows what the One-Degree Rule is and that they will be expected to talk about how they are taking steps to increase their personal temperature. They will also have a chance to strategize with the rest of the leaders about how they can raise the church temperature by another degree. How would this type of personal accountability impact the leadership culture of your church?

At Shoreline Community Church, every member of our Outreach Influence Team (staff and volunteer) knows that once a month they will be asked these questions. This is a powerful motivating factor which keeps our leaders accountable to the outreach vision.

As we look at the life and ministry of Jesus, we find that he too put great effort into holding his disciples accountable in this area. In the Gospel of Matthew, we read, "Jesus went through all the towns and villages, teaching in their synagogues, preaching the good news of the kingdom and healing every disease and sickness. When he saw the crowds, he had compassion on them, because they were harassed and helpless, like sheep without a shepherd. Then he said to his disciples, 'The harvest is plentiful but the workers are few. Ask the Lord of the harvest, therefore, to send out workers into his harvest field.'"[2] This passage presents us with a sobering reality: the problem in the evangelistic equation is not with the world and those who are spiritually wandering; it's with those who already are in God's family. Jesus wants us to see that there are many people who are hungry for God, but there are not enough workers reaching out.

Why?

I believe it's because our hearts have grown cold. We don't naturally share our faith or pray with the passion we should. Jesus tells us that we should pray — for ourselves and for the church. We need to toss a few more logs onto the fire to get it burning hotter.

RAISING THE TEMPERATURE OF YOUR CHURCH OR MINISTRY

There are many ways to turn the temperature up one more degree in your church or ministry.

Celebration

Jesus told three consecutive outreach parables about a found sheep, a found coin, and a son who wanders away and finally comes home to the loving arms of a waiting father.[3] What do these stories have in common?

Something lost is found, and at the end of the story, there is a party! The celebrations in these stories all point us to a simple spiritual reality that should lead us to celebrate every time a person comes to faith in Jesus.[4] When someone turns from sin to God, it should lead us to rejoice.

One great way to raise the outreach temperature in your church by one more degree is to plan regular celebrations of those who have repented of sin, left their old lives, and entered a joyful friendship with Jesus Christ. This can be done as a whole church at the time of baptism or through public declarations of faith. One way to build a bridge at these times is to be sure that the people making a public step of faith are encouraged to invite their nonbelieving friends to attend. It is natural to share the gospel in these settings. Celebrations like this should feel like a party! Have cake. Make it fun.

It can also be meaningful to have specific ministries hold their own celebrations of decisions for Christ. The children's ministry can plan a special event to rejoice over the young people who have committed their lives to following Jesus. This can become a pattern for any ministry in the church. We can't overcelebrate. The angels of heaven are having a party; we should join in the rejoicing.

Accountability

One of the most effective ways to keep the outreach fires burning hot is to create a culture of accountability. Believers should talk about their involvement in outreach. People should ask one another about their outreach temperature. We can inspire one another with good questions that spark conversations that turn things up another degree.

Here are some questions that Christians should ask one another on a regular basis:

- Who are you praying for who is not yet a follower of Jesus? How can I support you in prayer?
- Who are you spending time with who needs to know God's love and grace?
- Tell me about someone you are hoping will come to church with you sometime in the future.

- What is your outreach temperature in this season of life, and what are you doing to turn it up one degree?
- If you serve in a ministry area together, ask, What is our ministry temperature, and what can we do to help fan the flames and raise it another degree?

In a culture of mutual encouragement and accountability, these questions don't feel forced; they can happen spontaneously as we talk with others. They can also be woven into the leadership culture of the church. When groups of leaders and volunteers in the church are together, putting questions like this on the agenda can be a great way of keeping the fires burning hot.

Prayer

There is more power in prayer than we dream or imagine. I guarantee that the flames of outreach will grow hotter in your ministry after you make evangelistic prayer a normal part of your time together. Table 3 gives you some ideas for fueling outreach fires through prayer.

Ideas for Fueling Outreach Fires through Prayer

Pray as a congregation in worship services	• For each person in your church to love your community and serve people joyfully. • For healing in broken families, jobs for the unemployed, economic hope, and the needs that are on people's hearts. Ask God to help people see that the answers to these prayers come from his loving hand. • For hearts so in love with God and with people that we naturally share the joy and hope that are found in Jesus alone.
Pray as ministry teams, as a board, and as a staff anytime you gather	• For God to send workers into his harvest fields. This is the way Jesus taught us to pray (Matt. 9:38). Ask God to stir all of your church members to go into the world with his love and message. • For the people in your community to be drawn to the heart of God and to your church or to other Bible-teaching congregations in your community. • For a powerful revival, led by the Holy Spirit of God, in your community and in our world.

table 3

Proximity

The outreach temperature of any ministry will go up when we are engaging people who are far from God. It's all a matter of proximity. We need to move the church out into our community. In our personal lives, we need to be committed to make time, on a regular basis, to be with family and friends who are far from God. And in our ministry to others, we need to seek opportunities to get close to those who are far from God. Some of these people might visit your church, but many will not. Creatively find ways to get close to them.

This can be done in countless ways, and we will look at this more closely in part 3 of this book. Here are just a few ideas to get the juices flowing:

- A children's group can visit a retirement community once a quarter to sing praise songs or old hymns for those who live there.
- A youth group can serve meals at a mission.
- Small groups can support a family in the community that does not attend church but has lawn-care or house-cleaning needs.
- Members of a recovery group can offer rides home from a bar for those who are not safe to be on the roads.
- Men's and women's groups can spend a Saturday cleaning a park.

In all of these ways, and in hundreds of others, we will find our temperature going up as we come into closer proximity to people in our community, who in turn will get to know us and see that we really do carry the love of Jesus in our hearts.

Stories

Few things inspire us and increase our outreach temperature like hearing stories of changed lives. Every time we hear a testimony of God's power to save, we find ourselves wanting to be part of the adventure of evangelism. As a church, we need to create places for these stories to be told and heard, over and over again.

One way to do this is to have people share their stories in your worship services. This can be done by showing a testimony video, having a person read their story during a service, or conducting an interview. At our church, we share most of these stories of faith through video. We show them in services and then make them available on our website so people can watch them and share them with others.[5] We even keep these stories of faith online so people will be inspired for months to come.

Finally, we should seek to create a culture in which people naturally share their stories of faith. We should encourage people to think of different ways of sharing their faith in Jesus, depending on the circumstances and the person they are talking with. We don't have just *one* story of our conversion. We have daily stories of God's faithfulness and power unleashed in our lives. As God protects, leads, heals, and loves us, we can tell these stories.[6]

The Thirty-Day Rule

Everything that is important to a church is placed on the schedule and planned. I don't know of any church that just hopes someone will show up every week to take care of the babies in the nursery. No, we recruit volunteers, train them, and make a schedule. We don't simply hope and pray that a musician will show up to lead our Sunday worship service. We plan and practice to make sure we have a great worship experience that honors God and blesses people. In the same way, we need to plan regular times when we put new fuel on the outreach fire.

If it is important, we will make sure it gets done. If it is a high priority, everyone will know about it. With outreach, I have learned that we need to put fuel on the fire every single month of the year.

Yes, every month!

Vision "leaks." Even if your evangelism tank is full, it gradually drips away, and you need to top it off again. In most churches, the vision that seems to leak fastest is the commitment to outreach. After years of studying congregations and how they do (or don't do) evangelism, I have found that most church ministries lose their evangelistic passion in about thirty days.

If there is not a regular stoking of the outreach fires, it takes only a month for things to cool off significantly.

This means that a church that really wants to keep a healthy focus on reaching out with the love and grace of Jesus needs a spiritual infu-

128 of Your Congregation

sion of evangelistic passion every single month. Fuel must be added to this fire over and over again.

Some congregations try to have a yearly outreach emphasis. But an occasional pep talk is not enough to sustain a culture of outreach. Mentioning outreach in a sermon every once in a while will not get the job done.

The apostle Paul wrote, "Finally, be strong in the Lord and in his mighty power. Put on the full armor of God so that you can take your stand against the devil's schemes. For our struggle is not against flesh and blood, but against the rulers, against the authorities, against the powers of this dark world and against the spiritual forces of evil in the heavenly realms."[7] Paul reminds us that a battle is raging in the spiritual realm, and it spills over into our lives every day. The forces of hell are marshaled against the church. The attack of the enemy is directed against every believer who carries the gospel of Jesus in their heart and on their lips.

We shouldn't be surprised when the vision for evangelism leaks so quickly and the flames burn low after just a few weeks. The rulers, authorities, and spiritual powers of darkness are constantly shooting arrows at us, slashing with their swords, doing everything they can to tear holes in the outreach vision of the church. I know this is true because while most Christians and church leaders will honestly declare that they believe in evangelism, very few churches do much to live it out. Why? The enemy attacks, our vision leaks, and often we don't even notice what's happening.

Since the forces of hell are allied against the work of evangelism, we will need to dedicate an inordinately large percentage of our energies and resources to outreach. The fire for evangelism needs more fuel to keep things burning hot than any other ministry in the church.

The enemy will never stop. Like waves pounding on the shore, the attacks of our spiritual enemy are relentless. Day after day, he resists believers as we make an effort to press outward with the gospel. He throws water on the fire and tries to quench our passion to reach out with God's love.

What is the answer?

Despair?

Discouragement?

Wave the white flag and give up?

Never!

It is time for the church of God to stand up, put on our spiritual armor, pick up our swords, and fight back. We can't do this with an occasional outreach emphasis or a yearly missions Sunday, as meaningful as these might be. We must adopt a year-round strategy that will lift up the outreach vision, fortify the church for battle, throw logs on the fire, and mobilize God's people for the spiritual warfare we all face when we take the Great Commission seriously.

Each ministry of the church needs to add fuel to the fire of outreach on a monthly basis. Every Outreach Influence Team member and every Ministry Worker in the church needs an infusion of outreach training and encouragement every thirty days. Each ministry leader, along with their team, should determine how they will do this. Once a month the entire church—every area of ministry—should commit to finding a way to fuel the outreach dream. This is the Thirty-Day Rule. Lift up the vision for outreach. Celebrate what God is doing. Plan the next steps. And mobilize God's people to head into the harvest fields with the good news of Jesus. We must do this with relentless intentionality.

RAISING THE TEMPERATURE OF YOUR LEAD PASTOR, OUTREACH LEADER, TEAM MEMBERS, AND MINISTRY WORKERS

The Outreach Influence Team Leader

How does your Outreach Influence Team Leader raise his or her outreach temperature on a monthly basis? First, by spending time with Jesus every day. Though it may seem obvious, this is still the best way to keep the spiritual fires blazing. It is also the easiest to neglect.

Second, the Outreach Influence Team Leader must encourage the Outreach Influence Team members (including the Lead Pastor) and infuse them with new outreach ideas every month.[8] Perhaps you've heard people say, "I learn more preparing to teach others than I do sitting in a class." As the Outreach Influence Team Leader prepares and invests in the members of the Outreach Influence Team each month, this regular responsibility will challenge and inspire the team leader as well.

How the Lead Pastor and Outreach Influence Team Leader embrace and lead by example will set the tone for the entire church. To provide ongoing inspiration, accountability, learning, and planning for these two roles, Organic Outreach International provides an opportunity for thirty-day infusions through online cohort meetings. Cohorts are made up of the Lead Pastors and Outreach Influence Team Leaders of six to eight churches who meet monthly via online video conferencing. Each cohort is led by either a pastor or an Outreach Influence Team Leader who is either on the Organic Outreach International staff or has been certified to lead. These cohorts add the element of collaboration with other churches who are engaged in Organic Outreach and can be a powerful way to raise the evangelistic temperature of your Lead Pastor and Outreach Influence Team.[9]

The Outreach Influence Team

When the key leaders of your church ministries know they will be meeting with the Outreach Influence Team Leader on a monthly basis, this accountability keeps them fired up. Over the years as I've led several of these meetings, I have discovered a simple but effective rhythm. Each quarter, the Outreach Influence Team Leader plans three monthly meetings involving Outreach Influence Team members. Each of these meetings is unique and meets a different need, but they are all designed to put more fuel on the outreach fire. Every meeting includes the four key elements of inspiration, accountability, learning, and planning.

1. Full Team Meetings

Once a quarter, the Outreach Influence Team Leader brings the entire Outreach Influence Team together. In this gathering, each team member gives a brief report of their personal outreach temperature and their ministry's outreach temperature (using the One-Degree Rule—*accountability*). Sharing of temperatures brings sharing of stories. These stories of personal and ministry outreach encounters provide the critical element of *inspiration*. In the beginning, this time of the meeting will probably be pretty short and quiet. After several months, it will be one of the hardest parts of the meeting to keep to a timeframe! This is also a time for the Outreach Influence Team Leader to introduce a new Outreach Concept for the quarter (*learning*). Finally, the team will *plan* how all of the ministries of the church can partner for any upcoming churchwide outreach initiatives. During this meeting, every team member has a chance to share what outreach events, ministries, and training will be happening in their area of influence. Then the other leaders can pray for them and offer support.

If your church is larger, you could potentially have twenty-five or more ministry leaders on the Outreach Influence Team. With a team this large, it can be very challenging just to get through One-Degree checks and stories in the ninety minutes allotted for the meeting. In this case, you may consider breaking the team into two groups. You will still have the entire team together for the beginning of the meeting and then break into groups for the One-Degree and first part of the learning. One group can be led by the Outreach Influence Team Leader while the other is led by the Lead Pastor. Then the groups can come back together for the remainder of the learning and the planning portions of the meeting. This will allow for keeping within the designed timeframe without compromising the depth of sharing that takes place in the One-Degree and story parts of the meeting. Another situation you may encounter is that you actually have both level 3 and level 4 represented on the Outreach Influence Team in some cases. (For example, the Family Life Pastor is on the team as well as the High School and Middle School Ministry Leaders who report to the Family Life Pastor.) Breaking into two groups that are formed around level 3 and level 4 may be a great way to approach this if you have a larger team. Whether large or small, if you have both level 3 and level 4 represented on your Outreach Influence Team, it is important that the level 3 ministry leaders understand that they still have a responsibility to pour into and influence their level 4's even if they are on the team.

2. Strategic Cluster Meetings

Once a quarter, the Outreach Influence Team Leader pulls together smaller groups from the Outreach Influence Team. The goal is to meet in a more intimate setting to identify natural synergies and connections between ministries as they strategize how they can do outreach together. Every quarter, you can group the members of the Outreach Influence Team in different clusters so they can gain new insights and forge new partnerships. Here are some possible configurations for these cluster gatherings:

Cluster 1. Children's leader, junior high leader, high school leader, and college leader.

Cluster 2. Lead pastor, chair of the church board, chair of the deacons, and office administrator.

Cluster 3. Worship leader, lead pastor, and small groups leader.

Cluster 4. Small groups leader, women's ministry leader, and men's ministry leader.

Cluster 5. Nursery leader, children's ministry leader, and junior high leader.

The makeup of clusters can (and should) vary from quarter to quarter. However you decide to organize the clusters, think strategically. Imagine what might emerge when your leaders gather in smaller groups to focus on outreach. The agenda for this quarterly gathering of clusters can include checking in on personal outreach temperatures, sharing ministry temperatures, and identifying how the outreach flames can be stoked. Also, plan time for group members to discuss how they might begin working together and supporting each other in outreach. The key is to create directed but open space for prayer and conversations about outreach.

3. One-on-One Meetings

Finally, once a quarter the Outreach Influence Team Leader meets with each member of the Outreach Influence Team for a one-on-one meeting. This is a chance for each team member to receive some personal encouragement and counsel. It's a time to share concerns and ask for help, both in their personal outreach and in their area of ministry. The team leader can lead the monthly check-in on the team member's personal outreach temperature and the outreach temperature of the team member's ministry. This meeting is a good time for prayer and for casting new vision for creative outreach in the team member's area of ministry. It is also a wonderful time for the team leader to pastor these faithful and hardworking leaders. You never know what God will raise up in these one-on-one meetings.

The Ministry Workers

By now you are starting to get the picture. Monthly infusions of vision, energy, accountability, and teaching are powerful. They are also essential for the health of the church. If your Outreach Influence Team Leader is investing in each of the Outreach Influence Team members as suggested, they all will have inspiration and ideas to share with those who are serving in their areas of ministry. Ideally, these leaders will simply pass on what they are learning. Realistically, it doesn't happen unintentionally. When you get to the point of level 3 (Outreach Influence Team) influencing level 4 (Ministry Workers), it would be great if you could just replicate the structured approach of monthly meetings. At this point, however, most churches are really struggling just to get their ministry workers (volunteers) to commit to the hours they are already putting in. To add another monthly meeting would risk losing volunteers.

To overcome this, it is important that each member of the Outreach Influence Team develops a Level 3 to Level 4 Outreach Influence Plan. This should be written down, tailored to the ministry, and reviewed with the Outreach Influence Team Leader. Imagine the Ushers and Greeters Ministry in a church. Hopefully they are meeting each week five to ten minutes before they take their posts to pray together and go over any details they need to be aware of for that service. If the ministry leader asked them each to show up just another five minutes earlier every week, they could use that time to start their influence plan prior to prayer. The first week, they could go over the One-Degree Rule. (They could even show the video for this rule from the Organic Outreach International website.) The following three weeks, they do exactly the same thing, because volunteers don't typically serve every week. This way, after a month, every one of their ministry workers has learned the One-Degree Rule, and now they can take that extra five minutes to start doing temperature checks. Then tackle the Two-Degree Rule in the same fashion, and so on. While it will take much longer to get organic outreach infused into individual ministries this way, it can be amazingly effective, and it gets it done! One of the pastors of Shoreline Community Church in Monterey is a woodworker in his spare time. He started one particular project with enthusiasm when he had a couple of weeks' vacation. This was a very complex marble belltower with lots of moving parts and five different types of wood. He made great progress over those two weeks. Then it sat in his garage for four years. The problem was that while he had every intention of finishing it, he wanted to work on it only when he could get six to eight hours in at a time and could make substantial progress. After four years, he finally made up his mind that progress, however small, was progress. He decided that every time he had at least twenty minutes to work on the project, he would roll up his sleeves and do it. In two months, the project was complete. This is the approach ministry leaders need to take as they work on their Level 3 to Level 4 Influence Plans. True and lasting culture change does not happen in bursts and flurries. It happens over prolonged periods.

To help ministry leaders do this, we created Outreach Concept Sheets. These two-page sheets introduce a specific outreach idea, illustrate it from the life of the church, and provide discussion questions, prayer direction, and action ideas. The concept sheets provide a simple way for Outreach Influence Team members to train their Ministry Workers and can be used in a training setting or as devotions in monthly meetings.[10] Additionally, we have created some examples of Level 3 to Level 4 Outreach Influence Plans which can be downloaded from the website (www.OrganicOutreach.org).

· · ·

Do you see how outreach vision can spread throughout your church? By leveraging your ministry leaders and the natural connections they have with those who serve in their ministries, you can create a culture of organic outreach in your church. Your outreach leader trains other leaders, who invest in those who serve in their areas of ministry. In turn, these people have a natural impact on all of the participants in their ministry areas. Every thirty days, you'll naturally add fuel for outreach to every area of your church.

ORGANIC GARDENING

PREPARING THE SOIL

1. What is your personal outreach temperature, and what can you do to raise it by one degree?

2. What is your ministry's outreach temperature, and what can you do to raise the temperature another degree this month?

3. In a normal week, how much time do you spend with people who are spiritually disconnected? What can you do to increase this amount of time?

4. Who has God placed in your life who is spiritually disconnected? How can others pray for you as you grow a relationship with this person?

5. In your meetings, how might you add substantial discussion of ways you can reach out to your community with the gospel?

6. How can you help the Ministry Workers you partner with learn how to pray regularly for people who are spiritually disconnected?

7. How can you celebrate when there are conversions, when fruit is growing, and when your ministry is being effective in fulfilling God's call to do the work of evangelism?

SCATTERING SEEDS: HEAR AND SHARE STORIES

Share about how God has worked in your life or in the lives of others. Tell stories about spiritual conversations you are having, about conversions, about steps people have taken forward in their journeys of faith. Find creative ways to include these stories in your area of ministry.

SCATTERING SEEDS: TURN THINGS UP

Commit to raise the temperature for evangelism wherever God has placed you. If you are a leader, don't just tend to your own evangelistic temperature, but help others turn things up a degree too. Ask those you lead about their temperature, raise the temperature in your ministry area, and lead in a way that makes your area of ministry more effective in connecting the disconnected.

SCATTERING SEEDS: CELEBRATE

Commit to present a testimony of a life that has been changed by God's grace at least once a month in a worship service. These testimonies can be recorded and shown on video, presented as live interviews, or even read by another person. Create times when people can hear what God is doing and be filled with a desire to see more people come to faith in Jesus.

SCATTERING SEEDS: PUT OUTREACH ON EVERY AGENDA

Here is a simple way to keep people focused on the vision for outreach. Most ministries in the church have a team of leaders that meets on a monthly basis. Put evangelism on every agenda of every church ministry. And put it near the top.

WATERING WITH PRAYER

- Commit to pray three minutes each day for those God has placed in your life who are spiritually disconnected. To remind you, make a list, a note card, or a memo in your smartphone, and pray for God to draw these people to himself.

- Pray for your church leaders to be powerful examples of organic outreach. Lift up your staff and board members. Pray that the key leader of each of your church ministries will experience their outreach temperature going up on a regular basis.
- Confess where your heart has been cold toward lost and wandering people in your community, and ask the Spirit of God to give you new love for broken and spiritually disconnected people.
- Ask God to remind you, every thirty days, to do something specific to increase your outreach temperature.

Part Three

THE HANDS OF YOUR CONGREGATION

A church that loves people with the passionate heart of God will make a difference in their community and in the world. When the heartbeat of our church is strong, we will find ourselves growing in love with God, with the people in our community, and with the church.

As our hearts grow healthy, we can engage our minds and think deeply about ways that a church can take the good news of Jesus to the world. We think strategically and make shifts in how we do our ministry. We remove roadblocks to evangelism as we infuse the value of outreach into every level of the church. Then, as outreach fires burn hotter and hotter, our outreach temperature climbs. Once our hearts and minds have connected with the outreach vision of God, it's now time for our hands to get active.

We need to do something!

God's Word says it this way: "If anyone has material possessions and sees his brother in need but has no pity on him, how can the love of God be in him?"[1] James takes it a step farther with these challenging words: "Suppose a brother or sister is without clothes and daily food. If one of you says to him, 'Go, I wish you well; keep warm and well fed,' but does nothing about his physical needs, what good is it? In the same way, faith by itself, if it is not accompanied by action, is dead."[2]

Churches that want to make a lasting impact on their community will find natural, organic ways of serving as the hands, feet, and loving presence of Jesus right where they are. Changed hearts and minds inspire action.

In recent years, it has become popular to ask, "If your church disappeared today, would anyone notice?" That's a great question, but I would take it one step farther. Certainly, if a church is serving as the hands of Jesus in their community, everyone will notice if they disappear. But if a church is truly making a God-honoring impact, the community will do more than simply notice that this church is gone; they will mourn the loss of such a blessing to their lives.

Chapter Eight

The Two-Degree Rule

The Power of Vectoring

Many of your best outreach programs are already in place; you just don't know it! Your church is already doing all sorts of things with evangelistic potential. The problem is that we do most of these things for people who are already in God's family. The Two-Degree Rule is the practice of identifying what we do well and then turning our focus a few degrees out into the community and into the world, freeing our hands to serve those who are not yet in the church.

When a compass is working correctly, it points north. That's just how compasses work. In the church, our north, the default orientation of our focus and time, is to care for and minister to those who are already in the family of God.

I have shared this observation with thousands of pastors and leaders over the past decade and not a single person has disagreed with me. If left to their own devices, most churches will invest the vast majority of their time, resources, and energy in themselves.

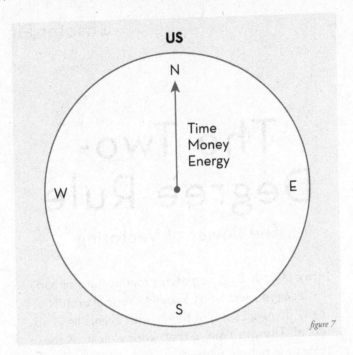

figure 7

This makes sense, doesn't it? The squeaky wheel gets the oil. Those who already know Jesus cry out the loudest for more attention and additional resources to be invested in them.

I have been a pastor for almost three decades, and rarely have I had nonbelieving community members come to me and ask me for my time, care, or ministry. Rarely do I get letters from people who don't attend my church asking me why my church is not doing enough for them and their families. On the other hand, I've received my share of texts, notes, and emails from church members letting me know exactly what they think the church should be doing for them. I find that I am regularly being evaluated by church people who point out to me, in detail, how they would like to see their needs met: the adjustment of our musical style, additional events for their children, sermon topics for me to address, or care for hospitalized family members. The list is endless. Most churches invest an inordinate percentage of their time and finances in people who already are followers of Jesus.

Not all of this is bad or wrong. I affirm that a large part of the Great Commission is that we teach believers and help them grow in maturity. Jesus told us that we are to *make disciples* and to *teach them* to obey everything he commanded.[1] As we reach out to those who are lost in the world, we must never forget that the church also exists to help believers grow into maturity in their faith. The apostle Paul set the bar high when he told believers that they should "no longer be infants, tossed back and forth by the waves, and blown here and there by every wind of teaching and by the cunning and craftiness of men in their deceitful scheming. Instead, speaking the truth in love, we will in all things grow up into him who is the Head, that is, Christ."[2] The church should certainly be in the business of helping believers "reach unity in the faith and in the knowledge of the Son of God and become mature, attaining to the whole measure of the fullness of Christ."[3] And this mission will require time, resources, and vision as well.

A healthy church is a church living with a profound awareness that evangelism (reaching the lost) and discipleship (growing the found) always go hand in hand. In light of these two key responsibilities, I'd like to suggest the Two-Degree Rule, a valuable way to unify the diverse ministries of your church. The Two-Degree Rule involves identifying what we are already doing for those who are part of the church and then finding creative ways to vector this activity into our community to engage nonbelievers. It's taking what we are already doing to care for, equip, and minister to our church family and giving it an evangelistic focus.[4]

The Two-Degree Rule is the idea that we can metaphorically push the needle of the church compass two degrees off dead north (caring for ourselves) to direct some of our resources, time, care, energy, and love toward those who are still far from God. This reorientation happens as we identify how we can take what we are already doing well and extend it to those who are spiritually disconnected.

UNDERSTANDING THE TWO-DEGREE RULE

After his death and resurrection, Jesus said to his followers, "Therefore *go* and make disciples of all nations, baptizing them in the name of the Father and of the Son and of the Holy Spirit, and teaching them to obey everything I have commanded you."[5] And then, just before ascending to heaven, Jesus said to them, "You will be my witnesses in Jerusalem, and in all Judea and Samaria, and to the *ends of the earth*."[6] Do you get the feeling that Jesus was pushing his followers outward, to the world? Like parents who prepare their children to go out and face the world as adults, God prepares us to leave behind the comfort of the church as we head into the world.

The truth is that many people in our communities won't come to our church campuses or buildings. They will stay where they are.

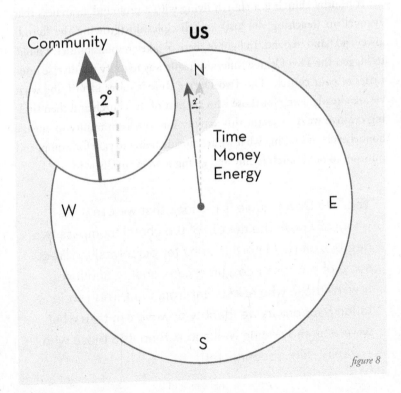

figure 8

That is why we must go to them.

Jesus was emphatic; we must *go* make disciples. We can start in a familiar place (Jerusalem), but if we follow Jesus, we will find ourselves pressing to the ends of the earth.

Why? Because that is where Jesus is going.

WHO NEEDS A MEAL?

For one hundred and four years, Corinth Reformed Church had a meals ministry. From its earliest days, this church was committed to taking meals to those who were in a time of need. If a woman had a baby or someone was recovering from surgery, people in the church would take them meals for the next five to seven days. This was a way for the church to show love, care for people, and simply be the body of Christ to each other.

It was a great ministry.

It was a popular and valuable service.

It revealed the grace of Christ and the love of his people.

It was only for members of the church.

One evening, as our newly formed Outreach Influence Team was meeting, we discussed the Two-Degree Rule. We talked about how we might take some of our existing church ministries whose compass needles were pointing toward our own members and reorient them a couple of degrees to include our community.

When I said this, one person excitedly suggested we consider the meals ministry. "What if we continued taking meals to church members, but we also made this service available to people in our community who don't know Jesus?"

Excitement filled the room.

The team members were amazed they had never thought of it before. They realized that we could vector this existing ministry out into the community. The ministry already had a successful history. Volunteers, leaders, and all of the systems were in place. As a matter of fact, one of the team members mentioned that some of the volunteers had been feeling discouraged because they wanted to deliver meals more often!

This was a turning point for our team. One of the members actually said, "Do you think it would be all right for us to have church members begin taking meals to people in the community when they are in a time of need? Could we really ask the church to look out for people in times of struggle and connect them to our church so we can serve them?" It was like someone flipped a switch and the lights came on. Everything looked different.

We talked about taking meals to single moms who are facing tough times. Excitement grew as we talked about people we knew who were facing surgery but did not have a church community to gather around them. One of the group members said, "I have a neighbor who never goes to church, but he has real physical needs. Could we take *him* meals?" There was electricity in the room as people spoke. Finally, someone joked, "We should have thought of this a hundred and four years ago!"

The first family in our community to receive meals as a result of our vectoring this ministry outward were friends of my family. They didn't attend any church. We had met when our boys were in the community soccer program. The wife was having surgery soon and her recovery would be very slow. My wife called her before the surgery and asked if it would be okay to line up five or six families from our church to take them meals on the days after she got home from the hospital. At first, she didn't know how to respond. Finally, she cautiously said, "I think that would be okay."

When she came home after surgery, people from the church extended love and care to her and her family by taking meals for a week. They were not pushy or aggressive. They just used their hands to prepare meals and then delivered them with the love of Jesus. The entire family was touched and blessed by the kindness of the church. Once she was up and around, she called the church and got the address of every person who had brought her a meal. Then she went to each home and delivered a little potted plant as a thank-you.

Several things happened through this whole process. Bridges were built. Friendships were forged. Service was offered. The love of Jesus was incarnated. And our church learned that it's not hard to take something we are already doing for ourselves and vector it a couple of degrees to also serve our community. That's the real value of the Two-Degree Rule: it's not about starting new ministries with new volunteers and additional resources. It's simply taking what you're already doing, something that is natural and normal, organic to the life of your church, and extending it to the people in your community.

MEET MY TWO-DEGREE HERO

Lynn Bruce is one of my outreach heroes. His story is filled with examples that can inspire people who want their area of ministry to become distinctly evangelistic. Lynn is a wonderful Christian leader. He loves the Lord and he believes in evangelism. But Lynn did not see himself as an outreach leader until he began applying the One-Degree and Two-Degree rules in his own ministry. And just for the record, Lynn was not at all excited about any of this—at first.

Lynn is a leader at Central Wesleyan Church in Holland, Michigan, a great church with an amazing heart for their community. Lynn leads in the area of administration and oversees the business affairs of the church. Most of what he does happens on the campus of the church.

When I started as the Outreach Influence Team Leader at the church, Lynn was already part of the Outreach Influence Team. Quarterly, I met with him in full team meetings, in strategic cluster meetings, and one-on-one. I was responsible for training him and helping him increase his commitment to outreach in his personal life and in his ministry.

When I first met with Lynn to talk about his personal outreach temperature, he was honest with me. His temperature wasn't what either of us would call sizzling hot. His wife, a naturally gifted evangelist, was engaging regularly in outreach activity, but Lynn's responsibilities at the church didn't naturally push him into the community. During that first meeting, he agreed to pray about his outreach temperature, but he admitted that he really did not see his ministry as having a great deal of outreach potential.

I listened to Lynn and then explained that his ministry had to be engaged in some aspect of outreach or it was not God's ministry. Over the next few months, we kept meeting and Lynn continued to work on increasing his personal temperature and his ministry's temperature. He was always forthright with me. He told me that he still did not see how outreach fit into his areas of business and administration. He talked about how the children's ministry, youth ministry, women's and men's ministries, and worship ministry all had natural ways to reach out.

But the ministry he did?

Administration?

Financial accounting?

The business of the church?

How could these ever be outreach?

After about six months, Lynn laid his cards on the table. He let me know that when he had been hired years before, it had been clear exactly what was expected of him. Now it felt like the church was adding on a new layer of responsibility and accountability in the area of outreach. He told me that it felt a bit unfair, a bait and switch. Lynn confessed that he had really given the entire outreach thing a good effort, but in the end, in a discouraged tone of voice, he admitted, "Nothing I do is outreach."

He meant it. Lynn could not see how his work and God's call to reach out intersected. I assured Lynn that every ministry of the church and every leader in the church had to be engaging in the work of evangelism. So we pressed on, and each time we met, we talked about the One-Degree Rule and how his personal and his ministry's outreach temperatures were doing. We also talked about the Two-Degree Rule and how he needed to discover what kinds of ministry were happening in his area of influence and then seek to vector those ministries into the community.

I asked Lynn to describe the ministries he oversaw. He mentioned a program for teaching biblical guidelines for handling money and stewarding personal finances called Crown Financial Ministries. This class had been offered at the church for years. As I'm sure you can guess by now, it had been advertised only to church members, those already part of the church.

After listening to Lynn, I asked, "Do you think there are people in our community who don't go to church who are struggling with finances? Could people in this community benefit from attending a program like Crown?" He laughed and said, "Almost everyone in our community is struggling, and they could all benefit greatly from the Crown Financial Ministries program!" This led to a spirited conversation about how he could make this program accessible to people in the community. Lynn committed to advertise the class in the community and to redesign it to make it more accessible to people who don't have a Christian background. He and the others on the financial ministry team reoriented their compass a couple of degrees, directing their focus from just the church to include the world.

After a year of meeting with me and working on the One-Degree and Two-Degree rules, as well as on several other outreach concepts, Lynn had an amazing breakthrough. Sitting together at a coffee shop, we talked about some of the vision for the church in the coming year, and as we conversed, Lynn began giving me an update on his ministry. I can't quote him word for word, but he said something like, "When we started working on this whole outreach thing, all I saw were obstacles. Now all I see are opportunities!"

Something in Lynn's perspective had changed.

Lynn went on to explain, "We are right in the middle of another Crown Financial Ministries class. There are four families in this class that do not have a church. I know it's not a lot, but four new families are coming to this class now to learn biblical truths for personal finances." I was so blessed by his words and energized by his excitement. Then he paused, looked at me, and said, "And not only are those families coming to the finance class, but some of them are coming to church too!"

I was blown away!

Lynn had worked with his team to vector into the community a ministry that already existed for believers. A few simple shifts had resulted in lives being touched by the message of God's love.

That wasn't all Lynn had to share. After giving this inspiring update, he said, "I am also responsible to help oversee the Crossroads ministry. This is a ministry to help people who are between jobs, looking for work, and who are facing a significant transitional time in their occupational lives. This is another ministry of our church that has been focused exclusively on believers. Now we are seeking to connect in our community through this program and are inviting other people to come."

Lynn went on to share how a group from the church had gone to a job fair in the community and distributed invitations to those looking at the booths and job opportunities. They simply offered people an invitation to the Crossroads gatherings, letting them know there was a free regular meeting of people facing occupational transitions.

Once he really grasped the Two-Degree Rule, Lynn started applying it to every area under his influence.

The Crossroads ministry already existed. All that needed to happen was for the leaders to think in bigger categories, vector into the community, and extend simple invitations. After telling me about the decision to direct the Crossroads ministry into the community, Lynn looked at me and said, "About half of the people in this ministry are now coming from the community and not from the church."

Lynn was not done. The same was true of the care ministry, which he also supervised. Lynn had introduced the idea that care team members could share their testimonies with each other during the training time for the ministry.[7] As members of this ministry shared their stories of God's presence and power with each other, something beautiful happened. They began talking about how they could share these same stories with people who are not yet followers of Jesus. The leaders in the care ministry naturally began vectoring their ministry outward.

Lynn was excited to let me know that three of the outreach concepts he had learned in our training were now having an impact in his area of ministry. Consider the change that God had brought about in his heart. Just a year earlier, Lynn was sure that his area of ministry had nothing to do with outreach. Now he was declaring, "Everything is outreach!"

A SHIFT IN THINKING, PROMOTION, AND ACTION

There is no simple, three-step process for implementing the Two-Degree Rule. But there are three ways you can help connect the ministries of your church with your community. If you take these ideas seriously and pray for the leading of the Holy Spirit, I am confident you will see many of your existing ministries transformed into opportunities to reach your community.

1. Think Bigger

Think about the people around you who are still far from God. When you plan the children's ministry schedule for the year, think about how your programs could impact the children of spiritual seekers in your community. As the women's ministry team thinks about new ideas and activities, they should ask, "How might we reach women in our town through each of these?" Make sure that every ministry is thinking about outreach at all times. Expand your circle from those in the church to include those whom Jesus calls us to reach.

It might help to put a note about the Two-Degree Rule on all your church ministries' agendas to keep this on their radar. As you do, your church compass will reorient a couple of degrees and the things you are already doing for believers will impact your community. When this happens, you will discover that your language needs to change. No more insider talk and secret handshakes. If you expect nonbelievers to be present, you will plan different, speak different, and make sure the message of Jesus is clear for all to hear.

2. Promote More Widely

Most churches promote what is happening within their circle of members and people who attend services and activities at the church. We use email, church websites, phone calls, Facebook, The City,[8] church bulletins, Sunday announcements, or other communication tools to let people know what is happening in the church. Good communication lets the people in the church know what is coming up, whether it applies to them, and how they can get involved.

The Two-Degree Rule moves us to ask, "How can we promote church events and activities in our community?" The answer is, "Lots of ways! Be creative." You can create invitations that people in a particular ministry can give to friends. Try using e-vites — electronic invitations that people in your church can forward to friends. Some newspapers and radio and TV stations advertise community events for free. Rent a billboard. You get the point. As you think about communicating what is happening in your church, widen the circle. If an event or gathering in your church might connect with people in your community, do all you can to let them know they are welcome.

3. Take Action

If you invite people from the community to a parenting seminar, a youth event, Christmas services, a women's tea, or any other happening at your church, be sure you have taken steps to make them feel at home. If nonchurched people start coming to any of your church gatherings, you need to be sure you create a loving and welcoming atmosphere. Have people ready to greet them. Give clear instructions so they don't feel out of place. Create a warm setting. Ask yourself, "If I were coming for the first time, would I feel welcome and comfortable?" Even making little adjustments to help spiritually curious people feel at home will make a big impact.

AN OKOBOJI LAKES CONFIRMATION

A couple of years after I began teaching the Two-Degree Rule to other pastors and outreach leaders, I had an opportunity to speak at the Okoboji Lakes Bible and Missionary Conference in Iowa. As part of this event, I spoke at a lunch for area pastors. I was delighted that close to a hundred pastors showed up, and I spent about an hour talking about organic outreach. They were excited, open, and hungry to learn.

After the lunch, a number of pastors came up to talk with me. Every one of them wanted to talk about the same thing—the Two-Degree Rule! They were excited and encouraged, and they loved the idea that they did not have to develop a bunch of new ministries or recruit new volunteers to do effective outreach. One by one they said things like, "We can actually do this. This makes sense. Why didn't I think of this years ago?"

Even before they left the lunch, they were already thinking of ways to apply the idea in their churches. One elderly Lutheran pastor told me,

"We have a church dinner every month. It is a great dinner. It is fun. And we have never invited anyone from the community." He looked at me with determination in his eyes and said, "That is going to change this month. We are going to challenge each person who comes to invite a nonchurched friend."

Another pastor told me that they have a practice of taking delicious homemade pies to people who visit their church. He said to me, "Now we are not going to wait for them to visit; we are going to take people pies before they come to our church." Pastor after pastor who talked with me already had ideas of how to vector what they were doing into their communities.

That's the simple power of the Two-Degree Rule.

ORGANIC GARDENING

PREPARING THE SOIL

1. What are you doing in your area of ministry that you can easily and naturally reorient a couple of degrees toward your community? What steps can you take to start this process?
2. How can you widen the circle of your communication to include your community?
3. What can you do to get all of your Outreach Influence Team members to use the Two-Degree Rule in their areas of leadership?
4. What are some of the responses you might get from longtime church members when you tell them you want to invite people from the community to be part of many of your existing ministries?
5. How can you help faithful church members see that including nonbelieving community members is a powerful way to fulfill the Great Commission?

SCATTERING SEEDS: EVALUATE EXISTING MINISTRIES

Look at every ministry you lead and ask, "How can we connect people in our community to this ministry?" If you can't find a way to vector this ministry outward, try harder. You will be amazed at how many existing ministries can be reoriented to reach the disconnected in your community.

SCATTERING SEEDS: COMMIT TO A BIG CIRCLE OF PROMOTION

Most of our promotion is in-house. We let the people in the church know what is happening (and sometimes we are not even very good at this). It is time to draw a bigger circle. When you are promoting a ministry, always ask, "How can we let the spiritually disconnected in our community know about this?" If you can vector the ministry outward, be sure to promote it as widely as possible. Many communities have free local papers you can use. Make your website friendly for first-time visitors. Let disconnected people know, "We are here for you!"

WATERING WITH PRAYER

- Pray for the members of your congregation to get excited about sharing the good things that are happening at your church with their friends in the community.
- Ask God to help your church love your community enough to exert the energy to reorient the church compass a couple of degrees off of "us" to include the spiritually disconnected.
- Pray for your Outreach Influence Team members to get this vision. Ask God to inspire their hearts to do all that is needed to vector their ministries out into the community.
- Pray that people in your community will accept the invitations they are extended and come see what is happening at your church and in the lives of believers who are part of your congregation.

Chapter Nine

The Value
of Innovation

Try Something

A church that wants to reach its community will take
risks, try new things, and seek innovative ways to
serve and build redemptive relationships with those
who are not part of the church. We need to be willing
to risk failure to discover new levels of success.

I was thrilled when I got the call.

Willow Creek Community Church was holding its first-ever event
on innovation in the church. They had invited around thirty church
teams to learn about a process developed by the IDEO Group, a process
that has been used to help many businesses and companies become
more innovative and effective.[1] The basic concepts they presented were
developed for the corporate world, but they transfer beautifully to the
church. The core ideas are quite simple: learn to innovate, try new
things, take chances, and be willing to fail. Doing these things will
give birth to new ideas.

Two world-class leaders walked us through the learning experience: Gary Hamel, considered one of the best thinkers in the world of

business today,[2] and Tom Kelley, the leader of IDEO.[3] Both men are brilliant thinkers and strategists in the business world. They also both happen to be devoted followers of Jesus Christ.

It's impossible to capture all that we learned during this two-day, hands-on learning adventure.[4] But the lessons I learned have inspired me to take more risks and innovate more aggressively as I partner with churches who want to grow and develop a biblical vision for outreach.[5] Here are some of the core ideas:

- We live in a time of rapid change. *If the church does not learn to innovate and change with the culture, we just might become irrelevant.*
- Many churches in America are not drawing people to Christ, not growing young people in the faith, and not becoming the world-changing institutions God intended them to be. *With wisdom and Spirit-led innovation, this could become a great moment in the history of the church when we see these trends change.*
- Most organizations are locked into a model and are not very open to change. This seems to be particularly true of Christian churches. *We must learn to identify where we are stuck and move forward with minds open to trying new things.*
- It can take a thousand new ideas to find one winner in the marketplace. This means the only way to succeed is to risk failing—a lot! *For the church to become more successful in the area of outreach, we will have to try a lot of things and be willing to celebrate failure and not be afraid of occasional mediocrity.*
- We can't innovate if we refuse to challenge our present way of doing things. In the church, this is hard to do because many people link traditions with doctrine. *It is possible to maintain and strengthen doctrinal orthodoxy and still question practices that no longer help us impact the world as God intended.*
- It is not enough to be an innovator today; we have to outrun the innovation trend. *The only way to do this is to make innovation part of our culture.*[6]
- We must adapt and stay relevant if we are going to survive and thrive. Dinosaurs became extinct. *If we love the old world so*

much that we never really enter the new world, we should not be surprised when our culture sees us as irrelevant.[7]
- Churches that lead the way into the future will be filled with anthropologists. We need to go into our community and see what people are really doing. If we love the world around us, we will study it closely. *We need to understand the various cultures that exist and learn about the ones that are emerging around us.*[8]

Churches that want to effectively impact the world around them will celebrate experimentation and nurture risk-takers. We must create an atmosphere in our churches in which people are free to try new things without fear of failure. Thomas Edison is supposed to have said, "I haven't failed. I've just found ten thousand ways that do not work." James Dyson, in the process of inventing his famous dual cyclone bagless vacuum cleaner, went through 5,142 prototypes. A church culture that encourages people to "fail forward" will breed experimenters who discover great ideas for God's kingdom. The work of the church is so important that we should be willing to fail, even a thousand times, if that is what it takes to succeed in taking the love of God and the message of Jesus to our world.

Even though these insights come from the business world, in many ways the work of the church — and especially the work of reaching lost people with God's love — has a unique advantage over businesses in applying them, because we know that the church is infused with the power of God's Spirit. Few of us will have to experience a hundred failures before landing on one good idea for outreach. As we take some risks and try new ways of reaching out, many of them will bear fruit. Some will not. But the process of trying new things and risking for the sake of God will grow our faith and bring glory to God. Our willingness to risk creates space for us to depend on God and his power. When we step forward in faith, God always responds.

TRY IT ON AND SEE IF IT FITS

All of us have gone to a store and tried on various items of clothing. Some were too baggy, and they went back on the rack. Some were too tight, so you kept looking. Some items of clothing looked great on the hanger or on a mannequin, but they didn't look as good on you. Thankfully, some things did look good—and they fit—and so you bought them.

When we try on clothes and they don't fit, we understand that we are in a process. The items we put back on the rack are not necessarily bad clothes. They just don't fit. When a pair of pants doesn't fit, that does not make us a bad person. We just keep shopping.

Understanding that innovation is a process is a necessary first step, especially when it comes to outreach. Have your church try on some new things. Give a new idea a month or two. If it fits, run with it. And if it doesn't, put it back on the rack.

WHERE DO WE GET IDEAS TO TRY ON?

There are all sorts of fun ways to cultivate innovation in your church. Rather than giving you a list of creative outreach ideas, I think it will be more helpful to tell you where to find ideas and how to create your own.

Borrowing

Don't feel like you need to reinvent everything. Find out what ideas are working for other churches and try them out for a while. Rummage through the closet of outreach ideas at a friend's church to see if you can find some you want to borrow.

- *Church Websites.* Research eight to ten church websites. Think of churches around the country that are doing great outreach ministry and review their sites. Also, see what churches in your region are doing. You will likely find a handful of creative ideas that can work for your church. In addition, be sure to check out the Organic Outreach website (*www.organicoutreach.org*), where we regularly feature new outreach ideas.
- *Magazines and Organizations.* A number of good outreach resources are available in print and online. I have been borrowing from *Outreach* magazine ever since it first came out. And for the record, they love to share. This magazine is loaded with

creative ideas for outreach events, programs, training, resources, and more. If you have a heart for outreach, get to know this magazine. Check out the Outreach Marketing company itself, which owns the magazine, as well as others that share ideas for programs and outreach ministries.[9]

- *Outreach Conferences.* A number of national and international gatherings focus on outreach. Most of these are annual events. I have attended the National Outreach Convention every year since it started. They have great speakers, practical seminars, and a huge room filled with some of the top innovators in outreach who are ready to provide ideas and resources to help your church reach people in your community. These numerous outreach gatherings range from smaller denominational events to large ecumenical conferences.[10]

- *Talk with Other Church Leaders.* Some years ago, I did research for an excellent book titled *Building a Contagious Church.* Mark Mittelberg, the author, asked if I could contact some churches to learn about their best outreach ideas.[11] To my surprise, as I contacted leaders at more than a hundred churches all over the United States and in other parts of the world, all of them were willing to share their ideas. Not a single church tried to keep their great ideas hidden from other churches. By simply setting aside an hour or so and calling or emailing some churches, you can find some new ideas for outreach, and even make some new friends.

Don't think you have to invent every idea. Be humble enough to learn from others, borrow freely, and have fun!

Old Faithful

Sometimes the best ideas for outreach are the programs that have worked for years. Innovation does not always involve embracing the newest and latest ideas. Some churches mistakenly abandon some of the best outreach ideas simply because they aren't trendy. There is nothing wrong with using an idea that has been effective in the past. If you have an outreach event or program that worked years ago, consider using it again.

Sometimes, an older program or idea can be freshened up with a new name, an updated logo, or a fresh presentation. You can even leave things exactly the way they are, if what you're doing is effective. It's up to you. But don't undervalue ideas and ministries that have worked in the past.

You might consider contacting a dozen churches you respect and asking them, "What has been your most effective way to reach out over the past ten years?" If these approaches have worked well for other churches, they just might work for you.[12]

Getting Innovative

To spark creativity with a team of leaders or church members, begin with a blank wall covered with paper, a pile of Post-it Notes, a bunch of pens, and a prayer. After you ask God to lead you, have people write down ideas to engage your community and reach out in new ways. Make it clear that there are no right or wrong answers. Give them freedom to be creative and dream. Have them write ideas on Post-it Notes and then stick them on the wall. Make it your goal to come up with a hundred ideas.

Then, have several people group these ideas by themes. Have your Outreach Influence Team see if there are a few they want to try on. Again, if something fits your church, wear it. If it does not, just put it back on the rack.

Some years ago, when Shoreline Community Church was just a new church, they came up with a creative idea for outreach. They started the Sunday morning service, sang a few songs, and then stopped for an intermission right in the middle of the worship set. The founding pastor, Howie Hugo, got up and said, "We have free coffee and donuts. Grab something, have a chat with a few people, and we'll be back to sing a little more in about ten minutes." One of the main reasons they did this was to further their vision for outreach.[13] They found that there were visitors who had been leaving after the service without connecting with anyone. The addition of an intermission early in the service made it possible for every person to make a couple of significant connections before the service was over. It was a brilliant idea that fit the church in its early years.

For outreach to be organic, the key is learning what works best for *your* church at *this* time. An innovative idea that worked twenty-five years ago might work again today. And an idea that was a home run just three years ago might no longer work. You need to use wisdom and discernment. You might find the ideas you need for the coming year at a conference or by borrowing from other churches. Or your church might thrive on getting a bunch of people in a room and dreaming up fifty, seventy-five, or a hundred new ideas.

Remember to Vector

As we learned in the last chapter, you can take most of what you already do for the believers in your church and use the Two-Degree Rule to vector these programs and events into your community. You might discover that some of your best innovations involve adjusting what you are already doing for those in your church to include people who are in your community. I have seen many churches add three or four new outreach ministries this way, and it did not cost a dime or another hour of volunteer time. They just needed to begin thinking in new ways.

The issue is not so much how or where you get your ideas. The key is that you gather a lot of ideas, try them on, and use what fits. What is organic for your church might not feel right for another congregation. Your church needs to find what fits and wear it proudly.

AS YOU TRY THINGS, REMEMBER...

Outreach is not a one-size-fits-all endeavor. As your church tries on lots of different outreach options, here are some helpful reminders to keep the process healthy.

For Everything There Is a Season

Innovation involves trying things. It also means there are times for certain programs, events, and activities to end. Shoreline Community Church no longer takes an intermission during the service. It worked well for a season and felt natural back when the church had a couple of hundred people. It does not fit who we are as a church anymore, so we stopped doing it.

We still have the same goal of making people feel welcome and providing space for them to connect, but now we serve a continental breakfast on Sunday—fifty-two weeks a year! We provide rolls, donuts, juice, coffee, fresh fruit, and oatmeal for about two thousand people every week. This is just one way in which we reach out—today. When this approach no longer feels like a natural fit for our outreach vision, we will stop doing it and try something else.

Sometimes churches have a difficult time letting a program die. They feel that ending an outreach program or stopping a particular event is a sign of failure. We need to be honest: if an event or program is no longer accomplishing the outreach goal it was designed to meet, it no longer fits; its season is over. Rather than putting it on life support, we should celebrate the great things that happened through this ministry and then let it die with dignity. All of us who serve Jesus need to remember that he is in the resurrection business. We might find that five or ten years from now, that old, dead ministry is just the right "new thing," and it can be resurrected.

I know some people who won't throw away their old bell-bottom jeans. They just know that one day they will be in style again, so they put them in the back of the closet or packed them in the attic, waiting to pull them out when the retro police declare that bell-bottoms are back in style. We can do the same with outreach ideas. If their season is over, we pack them away. Though they aren't a good fit right now, perhaps one day they will be back in style.

Innovate with a Purpose

Some people thrive on change for the sake of change. I was at a leaders gathering in Colorado when one of the pastors declared, "I love to keep people off balance. I change things in our worship service every week so no one ever knows what to expect." As he spoke, I felt a knot forming in my stomach. I wondered if he had gone just a bit too far with the idea of constantly innovating just for the sake of change.

We don't innovate just for the sake of doing new stuff. We don't keep changing things to throw people off balance. Instead, we innovate with a purpose in mind. If our goal is reaching lost people with the good news about Jesus, we pray, try new things, and offer all of our efforts to God. If an approach to reaching out works, we use it. If it does not, we move on. It is that simple.

Customize

Many of the outreach strategies, programs, and events you use will be borrowed. Some will be adapted from a past outreach idea your church used. In most cases, you will want to customize each to fit your church and cultural setting. Don't buy a boxed outreach kit off the shelf and unload it on your church as is. Your church and community are unique. You can use an existing idea, but make sure you customize it to fit the place where God has put you.

Over the years, my wife, Sherry, and I have written many small-group discussion guides. I can still remember the time we led a group through a study on marriage that we had written with Bill Hybels a couple of years earlier.[14] As we prepared to lead the study and reviewed the questions we had written, we tweaked a number of them. They were good questions, but they did not fit this particular group. We knew the needs of our group members, so we adjusted the questions to fit them.

In fact, I don't believe I have ever used a curriculum, study, or ministry resource exactly the way it was written. These materials are helpful, and I am thankful for them, but they are simply starting points, tools to aid in the work of ministry. We still must shape them for our unique ministry context. As you adapt existing outreach resources (including this one), pray for wisdom. As the Spirit leads, do some tweaking and shaping. The person who designed the idea was most likely a godly and wonderful person. But I'm certain they do not know your congregation and community as well as you do.

Try something new. Take some risks. Be willing to fail. It's worth it if in the process you discover outreach activities that will reach people in your community with the saving message of Jesus Christ.

ORGANIC GARDENING

PREPARING THE SOIL

1. Talk about a couple of outreach ideas your church has tried that just flopped. What did you learn from these experiences that prepared you for success in the future?
2. What is one outreach event or program your church has used that has helped people come to faith in Christ?
3. Is there an outreach program or event that you are presently using that might be coming to the end of its season? What can you do to conclude this approach and start something fresh and new?
4. Look at the list of lessons (at the start of this chapter) I learned from Gary Hamel and Tom Kelley. Which one do you most resonate with, and how can this insight help your church move toward being more innovative?
5. Why are churches fearful about trying things that might fail? What can you do to create an atmosphere in which failure is allowed and even encouraged?

SCATTERING SEEDS: DO A WEB SEARCH

Consider Organic Outreach to be a new operating system for your church. In this operating system, almost any program or app has a much greater chance of success than it would in an operating system that is broken or outdated. On our website (www.OrganicOutreach .org) we have a growing section of ministry partners who represent programs and apps that may be just right to thrive in your new operating system. In the coming week, in addition to reviewing these possibilities, take a look at websites of churches that are growing and doing effective outreach. Make a list of at least twenty-five outreach ideas that you think might work at your church. Share these with your Outreach Influence Team Leader. Encourage your outreach leader to share these with the Outreach Influence Team.

SCATTERING SEEDS: INTERVIEW LEADERS

Call the outreach leaders of five to ten churches in your area. Ask them what outreach strategies and programs are working for their churches. Invite them to share their insights on how they believe a church can be most effective in loving and serving its community in the name of Jesus. You might even ask them if they have any prayer needs for their own lives and for their ministries. If they share needs, offer to pray for them, and then thank them for their faithful service.

WATERING WITH PRAYER

- Pray for your church to be free from fear of failure. Ask God to give you boldness to take risks for Jesus in the area of outreach.
- Thank God for the people and programs that have helped your church reach out in the past.
- Pray for your church to grow in their commitment to innovation. Ask God to help those who resist change to grow more open, if the change will advance the work of the gospel.
- If you have outreach programs that have run their course, pray for sensitivity as you move beyond these old forms to some new approaches to reaching out.

Part Four

THE MOUTH OF YOUR CONGREGATION

The heart of your church is beating for Jesus and ready to reach out with love to the people in your community. The mind of your church is thinking strategically and planning to reach out with the good news of God's salvation. The hands of your church are working, serving, and showing the world that Jesus is alive.

Now the fun starts. It's time to open your mouth!

One of the greatest joys we have as followers of Christ is the privilege of communicating the message of Jesus to the world. We do this in many ways and often in diverse settings and circumstances, but the message we share should be clear and simple.

This is the good news we take to the world:

- God knows everything about us, and he still loves us beyond description.[1]
- Human beings have broken their relationship with God by rebelling against him and doing things that are opposed to his will. The Bible calls this sin.[2]
- God solved the problem of our sin by sending his only Son to pay the price for our wrongs, die in our place on the cross, and rise again to release heavenly power that sets us free. Through faith in Jesus, we can be forgiven, restored, and healed.[3]

- We can put our faith in Jesus, confess our sins, and invite him to become the leader of our lives and our closest friend. When we do this, we are born again, we are washed clean, heaven becomes our eternal home, and our lives on this earth have new purpose and meaning.[4]
- Once we receive Jesus as the one who forgives our sins and leads our lives, we begin a new adventure of following him every day.[5]
- As a church, are you ready to open your mouth and speak this message to your community? To the world?

Chapter Ten

Faith Comes by Hearing

Who Will Speak?

There are countless places and ways to communicate the good news of Jesus. If every Christian in your church is equipped and confident to share their testimony and God's story, outreach will be organic. The role of the church is to help all of God's people discover how they can naturally communicate Jesus' message in the many places God sends them.

When our hearts are beating with love for God, the world, and the church, we will naturally want to see people enter into a life-transforming relationship with Jesus. The Bible is clear: this can happen only when people hear the message of the gospel and by God's grace are led to understand their need to repent of sin, receive Jesus, and begin a whole new life. As we engage our minds to find new ways of moving the church into the world, we are also strategizing about how we can best help people articulate their faith. When our hands are serving in the name of Jesus, nonbelieving people eventually will ask, "Why do you care and serve the way you do? What is the source of this love?" These are the moments when we must be ready—and willing—to speak about the one who loves us and gave his life on the cross for our sins.

Organic outreach always leads to telling the story of Jesus. It moves us to share our own journeys of life and faith in Christ. As the Holy Spirit is leading our church forward in the work of the Great Commission, we should see more and more people naturally and regularly sharing the simple story of the gospel. It becomes more than something we know how to do; it becomes part of who we are.

Churches that engage in organic outreach prepare men and women, young and old, new Christians and longtime saints, to live as ambassadors of Jesus. As we've already seen, we must have love and a willingness to serve, sacrifice, and care for people in the name of Jesus. But these things—as important as they are—are never the whole story. At some point, we must also open our mouths and speak the words of life to people. We tell others about God's power to save, his amazing love, and the forgiveness we ourselves have received. We become ambassadors who can clearly articulate the message of the gospel, telling others that it is possible to be forgiven, healed, and restored to a relationship with the God who loves them through Jesus Christ.

In recent years it has become popular to quote an old saying: "Preach the gospel at all times. Use words when necessary."

When are words necessary?

The truth is, words are always necessary.

Our acts of love and service are powerful and can help open hearts to hear the message of Jesus, but faith comes by hearing the Word of God communicated with clarity.[1] For our outreach to be organic, naturally flowing out of our lives as believers, we must embrace our responsibility to clearly know and communicate the content of the gospel message. The apostle Paul wrote, "God was reconciling the world to himself in Christ, not counting men's sins against them. And he has committed to us the message of reconciliation. We are therefore Christ's ambassadors, as though God were making his appeal through us. We implore you on Christ's behalf: Be reconciled to God."[2] God wants to make his appeal through us, and this will mean opening our mouths and speaking the Good News.

THE CONTENT OF THE MESSAGE

The brief introduction to part 4 of this book outlines the basic content of the gospel message. It is a simple message even children can understand and share. Too often, we make things more complicated than they need to be. The good news is that God's love is greater than our sin. Through the life, death, and resurrection of Jesus, we can be forgiven of our offenses against God and made acceptable to him: "God made him who had no sin to be sin for us, so that in him we might become the righteousness of God."[3] The gospel calls us to confess our sins and repent—turning from our idols to trust in Christ—and promises that we will be washed clean and led into a glorious future that begins in this life and lasts into eternity. Ambassadors of Jesus take this message to the world.

There are many ways to tell this story and communicate the message of Jesus. In *Organic Outreach for Ordinary People*, I share how to engage in spiritual conversations, give ideas of different ways to share a personal testimony, and share some examples of different gospel presentations.[4] The key is realizing that there is not a one-size-fits-all approach to sharing the gospel. Each of us should practice different ways of communicating the gospel and find which ways feel most natural to us.

THE LOCATION OF THE MESSAGE

After Jesus rose from the dead, he clearly told his followers where we should take his message of grace and hope. He said to his disciples, "But you will receive power when the Holy Spirit comes on you; and you will be my witnesses in Jerusalem, and in all Judea and Samaria, and to the ends of the earth."[5] With these words, Jesus clarified the scope of our mission field. At Shoreline Community Church, we define the four regions Jesus referred to as shown in table 4.

The idea of structuring our outreach efforts in these four regions comes from Jesus' teaching.[6] Our Savior wasn't suggesting that we must start in our Jerusalem and then move progressively outward to the ends of the earth. People in the church can connect with the work of God in any of these four locations. What Jesus was saying is that our calling

Some Examples of Outreach Ministries at Shoreline Community Church

Biblical Location and Description	Contemporary Location	Some Examples of Outreach Ministries at Shoreline Community Church
Jerusalem: the disciples' home base	Our church campus and the homes of people in the church	• *Preaching.* Presenting the gospel and giving people opportunities to respond. • *First Impressions Team.* Greeters, ushers, hospitality (refreshments), information center, and all those who make that first contact with visitors to the church campus.[†] • *All Ministries.* If you are doing organic outreach, every ministry will present the good news of Jesus and share testimonies. • *Homes.* Training parents to partner in outreach to their children.[‡]
Judea: the surrounding community and region	The communities where people from our church live	• *Job Fair.* Partnering with local media and businesses to offer training and connections for job seekers. • *Community Halloween Party.* Free for all people in our community. • *Serve Saturdays.* Going out to do service projects in our neighborhoods in the name of Jesus. • *Strategic Partnerships.* Serving and supporting community events.
Samaria: the place and people that the Judeans often avoided	Places and people that are often avoided in our culture and even by the church	• *Convalescent Home Visits.* Taking God's grace to those who have limited mobility. • *I-Help.* Providing shelter for the homeless in our community. • *Women's Shelter.* Serving and supporting women in difficult times of transition.
The ends of the earth: anywhere outside the region of Judea	Our state, our nation, and the world	• *Missionary Support.* Around the country and the world. • *Strategic Partnerships.* Sending church people to Mexico, the Philippines, Guatemala, India, and other parts of the world. • *Relief Efforts.* As needs arise, sending teams to places like New Orleans to aid relief efforts, providing child support around the world, funding AIDS relief, and more.[§]

table 4

[†] One of the best churches to develop this idea is Granger Community Church, and you can learn from their story by reading Mark Walz, *First Impressions: Creating Wow Experiences in Your Church* (Loveland, Colo.: Group, 2004).

[‡] For strong resources on this partnership between churches and parents, check out Reggie Joiner, *Think Orange* (Colorado Springs: Cook, 2009).

[§] Check out World Vision and their programs for supporting children around the world at *www.worldvision.org*.

is right next door, at the ends of the earth, and everywhere in between. He doesn't want us to miss the different places and people that need the gospel. When our church is reaching out organically, we should be reaching people in all four of these regions.

One of my favorite outreach stories is about a guy named Bob. Bob was not very passionate about engaging in outreach in his Jerusalem, his Judea, or his Samaria, much less to the ends of the earth. With some coaxing and encouragement, Bob agreed to go on a mission trip to Mexico. It was billed as a work trip, but there were several opportunities for outreach and ministry in addition to the physical labor. Bob went on this trip because he is a carpenter and felt he could bring some expertise to the building part of the trip.

Going to Mexico (for Bob, the ends of the earth) turned Bob's life upside down. A fire for outreach was ignited in his heart while he was serving in another culture in a foreign country. Bob was hooked and began leading mission trips. He helped lead a team to Egypt, and again, his heart was broken and then put back together by the Spirit of God, with fresh love for the people he met who needed Jesus. Eventually, Bob realized that he did not want to engage in outreach only once a year on a mission trip. He began engaging in the outreach opportunities we were doing right on the church campus and in our community.

God is not concerned with where we start, just that we begin to engage in outreach. Bob first became God's witness at the ends of the earth and eventually engaged in efforts to reach out in his home church and community as well.

As you plan outreach for your congregation, be sure that you are creating opportunities in each of these areas: in your church, in your community, among people who are ignored or overlooked, and to areas outside your region or country (crossing boundaries of language and culture to share the gospel).

THE BEARERS OF THE MESSAGE

Is it possible for every person in your church to learn how to share the message of Jesus in a natural way? Many people are afraid of or repelled by the idea of doing outreach because they feel it always involves a confrontation with nonbelievers. Some Christians have been taught a one-dimensional approach to outreach that works best if you are an extrovert and enjoy confronting people. Because most people don't fit this personality type, they assume outreach is not for them.

Rather than reinvent the wheel, I'll simply direct you to the best book I've read for helping every Christian find their unique and God-given style of sharing faith. It's called *Becoming a Contagious Christian*. In this book and through related curriculum, Bill Hybels and Mark Mittelberg teach about six different outreach styles and how believers can be unleashed to share their faith in ways that are natural for them.[7]

In these materials, we learn that the Bible presents at least six styles of outreach: Confrontational, Intellectual, Testimonial, Interpersonal, Invitational, and Serving. As you think about your outreach programs and the events and training you offer, ask yourself, "Are we mobilizing people in a way that engages a variety of styles of outreach?" It's important to think about this and make sure we don't offer training and programs that appeal only to people who have a Confrontational style. Keep all six outreach styles in mind in your planning and you likely will see more people in your church discover that they can be involved in outreach in a way that fits who they are.

THE INTENSITY AND CLARITY OF THE MESSAGE

Some outreach events and programs present the gospel and give people an opportunity to receive Jesus as the one who forgives them and will lead their lives. Other outreach ministries offer a cup of cold water in the name of Jesus. Our churches need both ends of this continuum and everything in between.

At Shoreline Church, we talk about serving a balanced diet. This means we seek to have ministries and programs at each of four different outreach intensity levels:

Outreach Intensity Level 4. A direct presentation of the gospel with clear follow-up. This is the biggest, boldest presentation.

People are invited to come forward, meet with a pastor, receive a Bible, learn about next steps of faith (including baptism, growth groups, and personal Bible study), and we seek to connect them to community in the church. It is level 4 because it is our largest and most robust presentation of the gospel.

Outreach Intensity Level 3. Sharing the gospel through natural and relational connections. The presentation of the gospel is as bold and clear as level 4, but we make the follow-up a little less direct. Level 3 invites people to commit to Jesus, and then we connect them to next steps of growth by directing them to a Christian friend, a pastor, or our connections team. At level 3 there is not a walk up front and a team doing follow-up, but we facilitate natural connections.

Outreach Intensity Level 2. Acts of love and service that show the heart and presence of Jesus (clearly pointing to the Savior). In the church, these acts happen through many events, programs, and ministries where we expect to have chances to share our story (testimony) and the story of Jesus' grace. All of the people who serve in these ministries are trained to share the gospel and lead someone to commit their life to Jesus. They hope for and expect these opportunities because it is a level 2 outreach ministry.

Outreach Intensity Level 1. Acts of love and service that show the heart and presence of Jesus (with some connection to the church). These outreach ministries and events are similar to a level 2 except there is a hope, not an expectation, to share faith. Sharing faith is allowed, but often the witness of serving in Jesus' name is the main focus. Those who serve in these ministries are trained and ready, but they know there may be only occasional opportunities to share the story of Jesus.

On one end of the scale are ministries and events that have a high level of evangelistic intensity. I love these! They are opportunities to clearly present the message of Jesus and invite lost people to make a decision. They provide times for face-to-face counseling, opportunities to build a bridge of connection to the church, and ongoing discipleship after a person has received Jesus.

On the other end of the scale are ministries and events that have evangelistic power but are much less intense. We plan opportunities to exhibit in tangible ways the presence and love of Jesus. With acts of service, we build a bridge to Jesus and his church. These are times when we offer a cup of cold water in the name of Jesus.[8] In these moments, we are not preaching the gospel or calling for a commitment; we are simply serving and loving in a way that reveals the presence of our Savior. We are opening the door for conversations, if people are interested.

I believe churches should have outreach ministries that range from very intense to quite mild. In the following sections are descriptions of the four levels of intensity and a few examples of what we are doing at Shoreline Church. You might note that the various levels of evangelistic activity can happen in Jerusalem, Judea, Samaria, and at the ends of the earth.

Outreach Intensity Level 4

At intensity level 4, events and programs communicate the message of Jesus with actions and words. They include calling people to a public commitment to Jesus and following up with them to help them move forward in their next steps of faith.

Here are some examples:

- In some of our weekend services, we present the gospel and invite people to stand and make a public response. Trained prayer counselors are ready to meet with people and help them with the next steps of growth.
- We have mission trips on which we partner with local ministries to lead classes, children's programs, and services that present the gospel and challenge people to receive Jesus as their Savior.
- Our recovery ministry is an outreach that presents the saving message over and over and presents opportunities for people to receive Jesus and take the next steps of spiritual growth.

Outreach Intensity Level 3

At level 3, events and programs communicate the gospel of Jesus with actions and words. The gospel is presented one-on-one or in a group setting as a normal part of these outreach ministries.

Examples:

- We have weekend worship services during which the gospel is presented with clarity and people are invited to pray and receive Jesus. They are then encouraged to talk with a prayer counselor after the service.
- The team that participates in the women's shelter visitation ministry builds friendships and relationships over time. They are trained and ready to tell the story of Jesus and invite people to receive his love and grace.
- All of our church ministries, if they are using the One-Degree and Two-Degree rules, have spiritual seekers involved in their ministries. These are natural places to communicate the message of Jesus and for people to make life-changing commitments.

Outreach Intensity Level 2

At level 2, acts of love and service show the presence and grace of Jesus and allow participants the freedom to point directly to the Savior. Verbal invitations and printed information about Jesus and the ministry of the church build bridges to the church.

Examples:

- Our yearly job fair is a partnership with local media and businesses, but it is held on the church campus. People receive world-class training and also get to network with local companies. At the same time, our pastors host the event and have prayer teams available. Also, our connections center (information booth) is open with volunteers ready to build relationships with the hundreds of job seekers and vendors who come onto our church campus.
- Our clothes closet and food pantry are great examples of a level 2 outreach. Those who come to receive clothes and food

have conversations with volunteers who speak of faith, pray for needs, and share the message of Jesus as people express interest.

- Work teams have volunteered to do physical labor and construction work to help people in our community, in New Orleans, in Guatemala, and in other places of need. These acts are done in the name of Jesus. These acts of service also provide some opportunities to have spiritual conversations and to support local pastors and missionaries in their outreach efforts.

Outreach Intensity Level 1

At level 1, acts of love and service show the presence and grace of Jesus, building a bridge to the church and taking goodwill to the community and to the world.

Examples:

- Shoreline Church has volunteered to hand out water and offer other acts of service at an annual triathlon in the community and also at a national mountain bike event. These events need many helpers from the community to be successful. As opportunities arise, volunteers have casual conversations about why they are serving, about the church, and about Jesus. These conversations are not forced but happen naturally.
- We have cleaned up local parks, in partnership with people in the community, forging friendships and having many spiritual conversations.
- Just one last note. We don't do level 0 events or ministries. A level 0 is a situation where sharing faith is simply not allowed and never happens. If we can't find a way to tell our faith story or the story of Jesus, we don't invest the time and resources. Some people might disagree with this and feel that simply doing nice things is enough. We believe the resources of the church are so valuable that we must know there is a chance, at some level, to share the gospel or we simply don't engage in that ministry. There are churches that do lots of what they call outreach, but it is really community service with no gospel connection. I would encourage them to expand their menu to include the higher levels of outreach!

Having a balanced diet of all four levels of intensity is important for every congregation. If all of your outreach is only intensity level 1 and you never present the gospel, you will not have a healthy outreach ministry. If everything you do is at intensity level 4, calling for a response to the gospel, two things can happen. First, when you engage your community, some people will avoid you or not even invite you because your presence feels overbearing. You could actually drive people away. Second, many of your church members will not participate. Some of your church members need to begin with a level 1 event, and as they feel safe and learn that they can be part of outreach, they will grow willing to be part of events that have a more intense evangelistic focus. A healthy church plans outreach events and ministries that hit all four levels of intensity.

EQUIPPED TO TAKE THE MESSAGE

If we are going to encourage everyone in our church to adopt an evangelistic lifestyle, training will be essential. We can't assume that people know how to share their faith. To nurture an outreach culture in your church, you will need to offer consistent, practical, and diverse training opportunities.

The apostle Peter wrote, "But in your hearts set apart Christ as Lord. Always be prepared to give an answer to everyone who asks you to give the reason for the hope that you have. But do this with gentleness and respect."[9] We should be ever ready to "give an answer" to people. Why? Because hope flows through our lives. As people with hope living in a hopeless world, we can give others an answer as to why we have such enduring hope, and we can do this with gentle and respectful hearts. God wants us to be ready to express in words what we believe. Every Christian needs to be ready to humbly tell the story of Jesus.

Many churches offer training for their nursery leaders and coordinators. Some require yearly training that covers infant CPR, choking, safety, and emergency care for all of their volunteers.

Why?

Because lives hang in the balance.

Just think about it. We provide hours of nursery safety training, year after year, *just in case* a need arises. Some nursery helpers might go a whole year and not need the emergency skills they have developed. But if an emergency situation arises, they are ready. They are trained. They know their stuff.

If a church takes this much time to prepare nursery caregivers for a situation we hope will never arise, how much more should we prepare all of our members to share the life-giving message of salvation found in Jesus alone? This is something we hope they will do often and naturally.

Even Christians who read the Bible, love Jesus deeply, and care about lost people need regular training to share their faith. If we believe outreach is important, we will make every effort to equip all of the believers in our church for the ministry of evangelism, praying for opportunities for them to take the gospel to people. This calls for training at every level within the church. We typically do a great job in children's Sunday school, teaching the gospel and encouraging our young members to be prepared to share this good news. How often are we doing the same for the adults in our churches? Or for our ministry leaders and staff? The American Heart Association requires CPR training every two years to maintain certification. For most Christians it has been ten, twenty, or even sixty years since they have had training in sharing the gospel, much more since they have practiced it! At Shoreline Church in Monterey, Tom Green, our Outreach Influence Team Leader, has launched a CPR program (Christ's Presence Revealed) for our staff and ministry leaders. It began with our annual Outreach Training for the entire church, focused on sharing two stories—the gospel and our testimony (both conversion and day-to-day). In this training, time was built in for people to turn to each other and practice these stories with the person next to them (in five minutes or less). Following that training, every ministry leader was called upon in one of the Outreach Influence Team cluster meetings to share their conversion testimony and the gospel. Now every month in their cluster or one-on-one meetings, they know they may be called upon at any time to share again. Not only has this been a great way to "recertify" all of our ministry leaders, it has been an amazing experience for everyone in the Outreach Influence Team to hear the testimony of the others.

I encourage leaders to foster an environment that offers multiple options for training not just for the ministry leaders but for everyone in the church. Sometimes this will be done with the whole church in mind, but more often it is best tackled ministry by ministry. As in the earlier example of what it might look like to infuse organic outreach into an Ushers and Greeters Ministry, it is often done in small bites through the normal course of ministry, will vary widely from ministry to ministry, and will be tailored to fit each ministry's target audience. However it is done, it must be intentional and ongoing. Some ways to do this might be:

- Offer all-church learning opportunities through preaching in the main church services.
- Train through small group experiences.
- Include outreach training as part of the ongoing training of the various ministries in the church.
- Equip people through one-on-one mentoring.
- Offer special churchwide events.
- Hold an areawide outreach event, partnering with other congregations in the community.
- Take a team to a regional or national outreach event.

In the church, we emphasize anything we feel is truly important by taking it to the place where everyone gathers. For most congregations, this place is the main weekend worship service. I believe the best place to effectively train the majority of your people in outreach is during weekend services.

I have done this for several years at various churches. Some people worry that doing this will be offensive to visitors who are not believers in Jesus. I disagree. I suspect that most visitors know that we believe in Jesus and that we want the world to hear about who he is and how we can enter a relationship with him.

For three weeks each year, I turn the attention of the entire church family to reaching out to our friends, neighbors, and community with the message of God's love. If there are people in our services who don't know Jesus (and there always are), at least they will get a chance to hear the gospel. There is nothing wrong with that![10]

I pray that your church will begin engaging in outreach in new and powerful ways. God is ready to lead and inspire you. Be faithful. Be bold. Turn up the outreach temperature. Vector your ministries out into your community. Train your entire congregation to share the good news of Jesus.

Enjoy the adventure!

ORGANIC GARDENING

PREPARING THE SOIL

1. Why is it so important that you have the content of the gospel clear in your mind?
2. Share the basic story of the gospel in your own words with a Christian friend or your group members (if you are meeting in a small group).
3. How is your church engaging in outreach in your Jerusalem, Judea, Samaria, and to the ends of the earth? Do you need to invest more time in one of these areas? If so, what steps can you take?
4. Think about the four levels of outreach intensity discussed in this chapter. Do you have a balanced diet of outreach options? If not, talk about which levels of intensity you need to develop and how you can take steps forward.
5. What is your church doing to equip people for evangelism on a regular basis? What can you do to raise the bar in the area of your outreach training?
6. What are some of the barriers to getting a large percentage of your ministry leaders and participants to come to a training event? What can you do to remove these obstacles?

SCATTERING SEEDS: WHERE ARE WE?

Identify the regions in which your church is doing outreach. Use table 5 to help guide your reflection.

Biblical Location and Description	Contemporary Location	Examples of Outreach Ministries
Jerusalem: the disciples' home base	Our church campus and the homes of people in the church	
Judea: the surrounding community and region	The communities where people from our church live	
Samaria: the place and people that the Judeans often avoided	Places and people that are often avoided in our culture and even by the church	
The ends of the earth: anywhere outside the region of Judea	Our state, our nation, and the world	

table 5

SCATTERING SEEDS: MEASURE INTENSITY

Categorize the various outreach ministries in your church by their level of outreach intensity:

1. *Outreach Intensity Level 4:*

2. *Outreach Intensity Level 3:*

3. *Outreach Intensity Level 2:*

4. *Outreach Intensity Level 1:*

WATERING WITH PRAYER

- Pray that all those who are part of your church will increase their commitment to speak the words of life that are found in the gospel of Jesus.

- Ask the Holy Spirit to convict you and other church members anytime there is even the slightest compromise of biblical doctrine and the core message of the gospel.
- Think through how your church is reaching out in your Jerusalem, Judea, Samaria, and to the ends of the earth. Pray for greater effectiveness in each region that God sends you to.
- Pray that each person who is part of your church will discover and embrace their God-given style of outreach. Ask the Spirit to help each one find joy and peace in reaching out naturally.
- Lift up the leaders of your Outreach Influence Team and pray for them to live and lead outreach with growing passion and commitment.

Notes

PART ONE: THE HEART OF YOUR CONGREGATION
1. 1 John 4:8.
2. Deut. 6:5; Matt. 22:35–40.

CHAPTER ONE: LOVING GOD
1. Rev. 2:4.
2. Rev. 3:15–16.
3. Rev. 2:4.
4. Mark 12:30.
5. 1 John 3:1; 4:8, 16; 4:9–10; 5:2.
6. John 3:16.
7. Rev. 2:5.

CHAPTER TWO: LOVING THE WORLD
1. In a time when many churches are avoiding discussion of biblical doctrine, churches that want to reach out effectively will make sure they know what they believe and are biblical to the core. See chapter 3 of my book *Organic Outreach for Ordinary People* (Grand Rapids, Mich.: Zondervan, 2009) for more on this topic.
2. Luke 9:23.
3. If you want to study the decline being experienced in many parts of the American church, I recommend David Olsen, *The American Church in Crisis* (Grand Rapids, Mich.: Zondervan, 2008), and Bradley Wright, *Christians Are Hate-Filled Hypocrites ... and Other Lies You've Been Told* (Bloomington, Minn.: Bethany, 2010). I also encourage you to read blogs by Thom Rainer and Ed Stetzer on the topics of church growth and decline.
4. John 3:16.
5. Phil. 2:7.
6. 1 Peter 1:3–4.
7. Luke 10:25–37.

CHAPTER THREE: LOVING THE CHURCH
1. Rev. 2:4.
2. If you have heard people, whether inside of the church or outside, complain about how bad the church is, I encourage you to read this excellent book by Dr. Bradley Wright.

3. Rom. 12:4–6; 1 Cor. 12:11–13.
4. I mention this pastor, Harold Korver, often when I speak and write. His life is a testimony to the value of mentoring and influencing the next generation.
5. The apostle Paul uses the image of the church as a body often in his teaching: 1 Corinthians 12, Romans 12, and Ephesians 4.
6. Revelation 2–3.
7. Matt. 7:4–6.
8. Heb. 10:25.
9. If you want to learn some good lessons about how believers should use their words, read chapter 10 of my book *Seismic Shifts* (Grand Rapids, Mich.: Zondervan, 2005).

PART TWO: THE MIND OF YOUR CONGREGATION

1. Matt. 10:16.
2. Luke 10:27.

CHAPTER FOUR: SEVEN SIMPLE MIND SHIFTS THAT UNLOCK OUTREACH POTENTIAL

1. I have always been fascinated with the idea that little movements can have big implications. Several years ago, I wrote a book based on this idea titled *Seismic Shifts* (Grand Rapids, Mich.: Zondervan, 2005). In it, I looked at eighteen areas where a small shift in our spiritual lives can make a radical difference in our lives. This book was written to facilitate a churchwide experience spanning six weeks of learning on a personal level, in groups, and as a church. You can learn more about this on the Organic Outreach website (*www.organicoutreach.org*).
2. Matt. 6:21.
3. John Burke has written a wonderful book called *No Perfect People Allowed* (Grand Rapids, Mich.: Zondervan, 2005). It addresses this topic in detail and helps churches discover how they can create a culture of welcome and acceptance that allows people to come as they are and take time to let Jesus make them more than they ever dreamed they could be.
4. Luke 15:3–7.
5. Acts 1:12–14.
6. In my book *Organic Outreach for Ordinary People* (Grand Rapids, Mich.: Zondervan, 2009), I devote two chapters to the power of evangelistic prayer. See chapters 6 and 7.
7. In *Organic Outreach for Ordinary People*, I wrote a chapter titled "Embracing the Bible and Truth," in which I address the importance of an unwavering confidence that the Bible is true.
8. This story is used with permission and is a great example of how quickly beliefs can be challenged and abandoned. It is a great reminder of the need to teach doctrine in the church and to get people to be serious students of the Bible.
9. The *Becoming a Contagious Christian* book and training course are valuable tools that I highly encourage churches to use as they grow in outreach: Bill Hybels and Mark Mittelberg, *Becoming a Contagious Christian* (Grand Rapids, Mich.: Zondervan, 1996); Mark Mittelberg, Lee Strobel, and Bill Hybels, *Becoming a*

Contagious Christian Leader's Guide, rev. ed. (Grand Rapids, Mich.: Zondervan, 2007); Mark Mittelberg, Lee Strobel, and Bill Hybels, *Becoming a Contagious Christian Participant's Guide*, rev. ed. (Grand Rapids, Mich.: Zondervan, 2007).

CHAPTER FIVE: BEYOND PUSHPINS AND COMMITTEES TO ORGANIC OUTREACH

1. We found the two comedians we used for these events while attending the National Outreach Convention. If you go to the Outreach website (*www.out reach.com*), you can find names of Christian comedians by clicking on the Speakers tab.

CHAPTER SIX: THE SIX LEVELS OF INFLUENCE

1. Luke 15; 19:10.
2. Matt. 9:35–38; 28:19–20.
3. Matt. 5:13–16.
4. 2 Tim. 2:1–2.
5. 2 Tim. 1:5–6.
6. Luke 15; John 10:11–18.
7. Rom. 5:6–8.
8. 1 Peter 3:18.
9. John 16:7–11.
10. Acts 1:8.
11. Matt. 19:26.
12. You can find a detailed ministry description for the Outreach Influence Team Leader and several free downloadable resources on the Organic Outreach website (*www.organicoutreach.org*).
13. To learn more about these churches, check them out online: *www.faithchurch online.org* and *www.centralwesleyan.org*.
14. 1 Cor. 11:1.
15. 1 Peter 3:15.
16. Matt. 5:13–16.
17. In an address to pastors given in March of 2011, Ed Stetzer pointed out that a Barna Research Group study indicated that in 2006 about 4 percent of Christians identified themselves as having the gift of evangelism. This dropped to only 1 percent in 2011. See *http://www.westernrecorder.org/ recent-kentuck-news/538-work-in-evangelistic-ways*.
18. As I have preached at churches around the country, I have seen the growth of what I call the "green room phenomenon." This is a term I use for larger churches that have a special room for worship teams, leaders, and pastors to hang out in before and after worship services. It is a nice idea for people who are serving in multiple services. But I give this warning: make sure it does not become an easy way to avoid interaction with the body of Christ and church visitors. At Shoreline Church, I require all musicians and vocalists to be in at least one service, worshiping with the congregation. My wife, Sherry, and I sit with the congregation through all of our services. It allows us to connect with church members and with visitors.

19. The tools your Outreach Influence Team members need to coach and train their Ministry Workers monthly are provided as a free resource on the Organic Outreach website (*www.organicoutreach.org*). The Organic Outreach website has three years of agendas for Outreach Influence Team meetings, twelve Outreach Concept Sheets for training your leaders, and lots of video resources.

CHAPTER SEVEN: RAISING THE EVANGELISTIC TEMPERATURE

1. In *Organic Outreach for Ordinary People* (Grand Rapids, Mich.: Zondervan, 2009), I spend the entire fourth chapter helping individuals identify their personal outreach temperature. In addition, I look at numerous ways to increase your personal outreach temperature by one degree.
2. Matt. 9:35–38.
3. Luke 15.
4. Luke 15:7, 10, 32.
5. Check out the stories on Shoreline's website, *www.shorlinechurch.org*. You can also check out testimonies and videos from the church on our Vimeo site. Just go to Vimeo and search for "Shoreline Community Church Monterey."
6. This concept is so valuable that I devoted an entire chapter to telling stories of faith in *Organic Outreach for Ordinary People*. See chapter 12.
7. Eph. 6:10–12.
8. On the Organic Outreach website (*www.organicoutreach.org*) you can find free downloads of agendas for three years of monthly Outreach Influence Team meetings.
9. For details on joining a cohort, see www.organicoutreach.org.
10. These resources can be found on the Organic Outreach website (*www.organicoutreach.org*).

PART THREE: THE HANDS OF YOUR CONGREGATION

1. 1 John 3:17.
2. James 2:15–17.

CHAPTER EIGHT: THE TWO-DEGREE RULE

1. Matt. 28:19–20.
2. Eph. 4:14–15.
3. Eph. 4:13.
4. You can find a video teaching about the Two-Degree Rule on the Organic Outreach website (*www.organicoutreach.org*).
5. Matt. 28:19–20 (emphasis added).
6. Acts 1:8 (emphasis added).
7. For more information on sharing testimonies and stories of faith, see chapter 12 of *Organic Outreach for Ordinary People* (Grand Rapids, Mich.: Zondervan, 2009).
8. The City is a tool that builds natural communication and connections between the people in your church. See *www.onthecity.org* to learn more.

CHAPTER NINE: THE VALUE OF INNOVATION

1. I encourage you to take a little time to do a search on "IDEO Group" and learn more about this unique innovation company.
2. Learn more about Gary Hamel at his website (*www.garyhamel.com*). Be sure to check out his books, especially Gary Hamel, *Leading the Revolution* (New York: Plume, 2002) and Gary Hamel and C. K. Prahalad, *Competing for the Future* (Boston: Harvard Business School Press, 1996). Great stuff!
3. If you search on "Tom Kelley books," you will find a wealth of learning on innovation. In particular, I recommend his books *The Ten Faces of Innovation* (New York: Doubleday, 2005) and *The Art of Innovation* (New York: Doubleday, 2001).
4. Willow Creek is developing resources based on this learning experience. You can find them on their website (*www.willowcreek.com*). You can also check out the video we developed at Shoreline Church to share the story of how we are using this innovative process in our church. Go to Vimeo and search on "Shoreline Community Church Monterey."
5. I give full credit to Gary Hamel and Tom Kelley for the ideas presented in this section.
6. Tom calls this the Red Queen Effect.
7. In his books, Tom deals with some examples in the business world. The case studies he presents, ranging from tire companies to Kodak, are fascinating.
8. These are just a few of the insights discussed in Tom's book *The Ten Faces of Innovation*.
9. As you are searching online for ideas, be sure to look for organizations and magazines that focus on outreach for children, teens, women, men, and any other group in your church. There is a wealth of ideas for free on the internet.
10. Events like the National Outreach Convention are very valuable. But don't miss some of the smaller events and denominational gatherings. The Organic Outreach Conference will be a great option, and you can find local and national evangelism gatherings with a quick web search. Also, some leaders events will have an outreach track. Check these out as well.
11. The current edition of this book, which was revised in 2007 and retitled *Becoming a Contagious Church*, does not have the six chapters on outreach styles and all of the examples found in the original book. You might want to go online and search for the original edition: Mark Mittelberg, with contributions by Bill Hybels, *Building a Contagious Church* (Grand Rapids, Mich.: Zondervan, 2001).
12. If you do this kind of research, be sure to share your ideas and learnings with other leaders and churches. God rejoices when believers work together!
13. Howie Hugo tried all sorts of innovative ideas. He could write a book on things that worked and ideas that flopped. He and the church leaders dared to try things that might fail.
14. The *Interactions* and *New Community* small group series each have twenty-four small group books covering a variety of topics.

PART FOUR: THE MOUTH OF YOUR CONGREGATION

1. Ps. 86:15; 1 John 3:1.
2. Rom. 3:23; 6:23.

3. John 3:16; 1 John 4:10.
4. 1 John 1:9; Ps. 103:12; Rom. 10:9–10.
5. Rom. 12:1–3.

CHAPTER TEN: FAITH COMES BY HEARING

1. Rom. 10:16–18.
2. 2 Cor. 5:19–20.
3. 2 Cor. 5:21.
4. See chapters 11, 12, and 13 of *Organic Outreach for Ordinary People* (Grand Rapids, Mich.: Zondervan, 2009).
5. Acts 1:8.
6. I never really connected with how this would be a valuable way to organize outreach ministries until the missions pastor at Corinth Church made a diagram illustrating table 4. Coincidentally, the person who taught me to take these four regions of influence seriously is one of the editors of this book, Ryan Pazdur.
7. *Becoming a Contagious Christian* is a book (Grand Rapids, Mich.: Zondervan, 1996) and a curriculum (Grand Rapids, Mich.: Zondervan, 2007). If you have not used either of these at your church, review them and see if they fit you.
8. Matt. 10:42.
9. 1 Peter 3:15. Check out resources like Bill Hybels, *Just Walk across the Room* (Grand Rapids, Mich.: Zondervan, 2006); the *Organic Outreach* campaign (*www.organicoutreach.org*); D. James Kennedy, *Evangelism Explosion*, 4th ed., rev. (Wheaton, Ill.: Tyndale, 1996); Bill Hybels and Mark Mittelberg, *Becoming a Contagious Christian* (Grand Rapids, Mich.: Zondervan, 1996); and Bill Hybels, with Kevin Harney and Sherry Harney, *Reaching Out: Sharing God's Love Naturally*, updated ed. (Grand Rapids, Mich.: Zondervan, 2005), a small group study.
10. I am so committed to this kind of training that I have designed a three-week churchwide experience to walk a congregation through the core lessons of organic outreach. This series includes sermons, small group resources, a Bible reading guide, original videos, and lots of other resources, all of which are available for free on the Organic Outreach website (*www.organicoutreach.org*).

OrganicOutreach

INTERNATIONAL

Through training, coaching, and provision of resources, Organic Outreach International is committed to helping denominations, national groups, regional movements, parachurch organizations, and local churches around the world infuse the DNA of their ministries and congregations with a passion for natural evangelism. We offer online and onsite training sessions ranging from half-day introductory seminars to two-day Intensive Trainings. For churches and movements that are directly engaging in organic outreach, we provide a collaborative coaching experience for small groups (cohorts) of pastors and Outreach Influence Team Leaders through a combination of online work and monthly video-conferencing.

For churches and organizations engaging in organic outreach, we provide free resources on our website. As you browse through this library, you will find a full three years of Outreach Influence Team meeting agendas, samples of Level 3 to Level 4 Influence plans, an Outreach Influence Team Leader ministry description, training and informational videos, and more. We are constantly updating and adding to these tools, so check back often.

You can contact the OOI team through the website (www.Organic Outreach.org) or by email (info@OrganicOutreach.org).

Organic Outreach International is a ministry of Shoreline Community Church in Monterey, California.

Simple, Natural Ways to Share Your Faith

ZONDERVAN®